CRITICISMS OF LIFE
STUDIES IN FAITH, HOPE, AND DESPAIR

CRITICISMS OF LIFE

STUDIES IN FAITH, HOPE
AND DESPAIR

BY
HORACE J. BRIDGES

8 1 4
1376

BOSTON AND NEW YORK
HOUGHTON MIFFLIN COMPANY
The Riverside Press Cambridge
MDCCCCXV

TO MY SPIRITUAL FATHER
STANTON COIT
IN GLAD ACKNOWLEDGMENT
OF AN ETERNAL DEBT

52016

" Why dost thou wonder, O Man, at the height of the stars or the depth of the sea? Enter into thine own soul, and wonder there "

CONTENTS

INTRODUCTION

THE eight studies which make up the present volume are intended primarily as illustrations of the faith and hope by which men actually live to-day. In those covered by the term "Despair" in the title, the purpose has been not merely to criticize the doctrines rejected, but to justify faith and hope by destroying the grounds of their opposites.

It is the writer's belief that the principles which he has endeavoured partially to set forth, though they are not as yet embodied in the formal creed of any Church, and indeed are in radical conflict with many accepted ecclesiastical doctrines, are nevertheless principles which do in fact regulate the action of ever-widening circles of mankind.

We are accustomed to a somewhat superficial antithesis between creed and conduct. We commonly hear men spoken of as being "better than their creed." The antithesis has been formulated by Mr. Bernard Shaw in the statement that "What a man believes may be ascertained, not from his creed, but from the assumptions on which he habitually acts." This, however, is merely a slapdash, journalistic way of speaking. The fallacy it contains becomes self-evident the moment we substitute for the Latin word "creed" its English equivalent. If we do this, Mr. Shaw's statement will run, "What a man believes may be ascertained, not from his belief, but from the assumptions on which he habitually acts." Quite evidently, this will not do; but it enables us to see and state the truth which Mr. Shaw has aimed at and missed. The assumptions on which a man habitually acts *are* his creed; and if he professes to believe doctrines incompatible with these assumptions, he misunderstands himself.

Now, my contention is that large numbers of perfectly sincere religious people are to-day mistaken as to their real creed. They have inherited the doctrines of a pre-democratic, pre-scientific, and therefore supernaturalistic age, and they have failed to detect the fact that the whole of our modern life is animated and guided by inevitable presuppositions which are fundamentally at variance with those that engendered the time-honoured statements of the ancient Confessions. It is not so much that our new knowledge of the facts of life has made it difficult for us to believe in miracles and in the arbitrary providence of an outside God, but rather that the practical exigencies of life — the concrete experience of the nations of Christendom through the centuries in which democracy and science have been hewn out — have forced us to act upon the assumption that there is no intelligent or providential interference with the order of nature except that of living human beings.

One need not be a Pragmatist to see that it is experience which leads to the *discovery* of truth. I do not
affirm that truth is merely that which "works," or
that everything which "works" is truth. No doubt
things are true before they are found to "work," and
therefore that which makes them true must be defined
otherwise than by the fact that they do so. My point
here is only that we are led to the discernment of truth
by the exigencies of personal and social life. Now, we
find that the civilized nations of the world to-day, even
though they still pay abundant lip-service to super-
naturalism and to the doctrine of miracles, act continuously and unhesitatingly upon the assumptions that,
apart from the human will, nothing ever happens
except in terms of the law of causation, which is coextensive not only with all actual but with all possible
experience, and that miracle is incompatible with the
very existence of human society. We are therefore
entitled to say that these two principles form part
of the real creed of Christendom, and that the day
has accordingly come when everything in its nominal
creeds which is incompatible with them should be
extruded.

Another revelation which the experience of the ages
has at last brought clearly into our consciousness is
the truth that moral perfection is the only rightful object of human worship, and that it is equally worthy
of unconditional reverence whether it be embodied
in a superhuman person whose power is infinite, or

in the feeblest and least fortunately circumstanced of human beings. This teaching is not so much a new theory which innovating liberal Churches (like the Ethical Societies) have reached by a process of abstract reasoning, as a regulative principle which does actually animate all the moral judgments, even of those whose formal theology repudiates it. It is of the essence not only of morality but of democracy. The doctrine of human equality, which, in a Republic like the United States, is universally accepted, can never be justified except upon this inevitable practical assumption. The Ethical Societies, therefore, in asserting the supremacy of the Moral Ideal as "God above all gods worshipped of all nations," and in declaring that no being, natural or supernatural, human or superhuman, is to receive worship except because and in so far as it embodies and illustrates the Moral Ideal, are but giving expression to a truth rooted in and vital to the essential sanity of human life.

It is in the light of these two principles — the principle of Idealistic Naturalism and the principle of the Supremacy of Ethics — that I have re-examined the special problems dealt with by the writers and thinkers whose works I have used as texts.

I shall probably not be called upon to defend myself against the charge of theological conservatism. On the other hand, the conclusions as to social ethics which I have set forth (especially in connection with the questions of Suicide and of Marriage and Divorce) may incur the accusation of moral unprogressiveness. I shall not shrink from this imputation, provided only that those who make it will do me the justice to remember that my conclusions are in each case based upon experience, and not upon ecclesiastical authority. It is my conviction that a revaluation of moral values, such as Nietzsche planned but never achieved, does not necessarily lead to a transvaluation or disvaluation of them; for I hold that many social standards and institutions which to-day are assailed as obsolete, merely because they are commonly justified on supernaturalistic or other unverifiable principles, are really rooted in the instinctive moral wisdom of man, and that the intellectualistic justifications offered for them were invented *ex post facto*. If so, these standards and institutions do not fall with their old defences; but it does become necessary to find for them a new theoretical justification, founded in the unassailable truths of universal experience. It is also necessary to distinguish whether admitted evils, associated with them, are inherent or due to adventitious causes; since in the latter case the evils can be cured without tampering with the essential principles of the institutions affected by them.

The teaching of this book represents my own attempt to apply the principles of the Ethical Movement to certain specific religious and social issues. For the faults and errors which it contains I am alone responsible, but whatever in it is sound and good I owe to my teachers and colleagues in that movement, whose influence through many years, both in England and in this country, has been to me an inexpressible blessing. It is not only a duty but a delight to me to mention especially in this connection the name of Dr. Stanton Coit, to whom, after eight years of daily intercourse, my debt is so inexhaustible that it sometimes seems as though I had not a single idea, aspiration or hope which was not the outgrowth of my association with him. Whoever reads his book on "The Soul of America," or looks through the vast anthology of Ethical scripture and psalmody which he has published under the title of "Social Worship," will readily detect the depth and breadth of my obligations to him. Nor can I deny myself the pleasure of acknowledging with equal gratitude the spiritual quickening and mental clarification which I owe to Professor Felix Adler, the founder of the first Ethical Society and of the international Ethical Movement. These two leaders, moreover, would be the first to admit that their thought has neither come to them unmediated from the infinite nor been evolved by themselves *a priori*, but is the mature expression of a social wisdom, growing out of their protracted contact with life in general, and especially with the organized groups to which they minister.

My book, accordingly (although the censure of its defects will rightly fall exclusively on myself), is in essence no mere individual utterance, but aspires to give voice to a growing synthesis of the common wisdom of a group of men and women who, sensitive to the spiritual trend of our age, have sought to give expression both to its needs and to its quickening inspirations, in order that the needs may be met and that the inspirations, becoming incarnate in the conscious will and purpose of mankind, may be made more potent and effective for the healing of the nations.

I take this opportunity of thanking my old friend and colleague Mr. G. E. O'Dell for his help in reading the proofs of this book, and for many valuable criticisms and suggestions.

H. J. B.

CHICAGO, ILL., May 5, 1914.

CRITICISMS OF LIFE

CHAPTER I

FRANCIS THOMPSON'S "THE HOUND OF HEAVEN":
A STUDY IN RELIGIOUS EXPERIENCE

EVERY preacher profits by the comments of friends upon his choice of themes. When, some time since, I announced a sermon on "The Hound of Heaven," one gentleman told me that he was at a loss to conceive how I could find in the poem material for a discourse. Another, a man of immense reading and of delicate literary and poetic taste, declared that, apart from its amazing richness of imagery and witchery of expression, he could see nothing in "The Hound of Heaven" except a deep and bitter sorrow.

These friends will pardon me for saying that their judgment betrays a singular obsession. It proves that they, like the mass of the uninitiated, are still under the hypnotic spell of the idea that religious experience is dependent upon, and inextricably bound up with, supernaturalistic theories of the nature, environment and destiny of the human soul. In spite of the researches into religious psychology which in recent years have enriched Anglo-American literature, — in spite of the work of Leuba, Starbuck, James and the

rest, — men continue to regard certain types of spiritual life as possible of manifestation only in conjunction with doctrines which are rapidly and deservedly
losing their grip on the mind and will of men. The implied conclusion — that, if this connection exists, then
mankind must for the future be deprived of blessed
and exalting experiences which in the past have transformed lives and inspired mighty deeds and marvellous literature — is one that they either refuse to face
or submit to as inevitable, even if regrettable.

The premise, however, is false; and the conclusion is
accordingly baseless. The error involved in both will
become apparent if we recall to mind two self-evident
facts which we ordinarily forget.

The first is this: that all human beings, whatever
their variations of ancestry, tradition, language and
immediate environment (psychical and physical), participate in a common nature and form part of the same
universe of actual and possible experience. Their identity is deeper and wider than their difference. Unless
we have carried pragmatism to the length of solip-
sism (the philosophical synonym for insanity), we can
neither deny the multiplicity of minds in touch with
a common reality, nor believe that the differences in
men's interpretations of the world correspond to actual
differences in it. For example, if one man says that
animal species were each separately originated by a
superhuman fiat, and another that their differentia-
tion is due only to efficient causes traceable in hered-

ity and environment, we agree that both cannot be right. By one or both of them, the facts must have been misinterpreted, or elements of explanatory theory unwarranted by the data introduced.

The second self-evident proposition is that, just as reality does not vary with the varying theories of different minds, so neither does it alter in correspondence with change in the particular theories successively held by any individual person. "Things are what they are" for rationality in general, not necessarily for your or my individual consciousness. Experience precedes interpretation, and is common and constant where interpretations differ. The mutually exclusive statements that the sun goes round the earth and that the earth goes round the sun are relative to an experience which is the same for both theorists. Or, again, I may interpret the thoughts, feelings and volitions in my mind as due to my conscious and sub-conscious self-activity; another will account for them by the suggestions of disembodied spirits, who practise upon me without my knowledge. For both of us the data will be the same, and we shall agree that the difference exists only in our interpretations.

But if this be so in general, how can we suppose that the case of religious experience stands unique and solitary in the world? Why in this one instance should the otherwise universal rule be reversed, and theory precede and beget that which it interprets? If in every other department of our mental life we find that the elements of fact are constant and only their theoretical counterpart in consciousness variable, are we not postulating unawares a stupendous miracle when we affirm that in religion there are as many different kinds of experience as there are theories, and no possibility of experience where there is no theory?

Surely, in regard to the life of religion, we should be led *a priori* to anticipate that there will be no complete and unaccountable difference between it and other fields of man's contact with reality. We should be led to expect very many common factors in the actual experience, together with many variations in the theoretical counterpart offered by different persons to interpret what they have undergone.

This anticipation, based on our general knowledge of man and nature, is confirmed *a posteriori* — by the facts disclosed through the researches of modern psychology. Consider the enormous mass of data which Professor James accumulated, and set forth, together with those he had borrowed from Leuba, Starbuck and others, in his Gifford Lectures on "The Varieties of Religious Experience." These instances, which might be indefinitely added to, demonstrate that the actual phenomena of religious experience are the same in all religions; they underlie every shade of belief and unbelief. This statement is the precise opposite of that which Mr. G. K. Chesterton falsely accuses some modern thinkers of making. He pretends that they say, "The religions of the world differ in rites and forms, but they are the same in what they teach." Nobody except Mr. Chesterton, the supreme genius of inaccuracy, ever said any such thing; but scientific investigation has demonstrated the fact that the widely differing teachings of the world's religions are attempts to account for a common experience, just as the ever-changing opinions held in successive periods by scientific workers are based upon contact with a common reality.

A man's experiences will naturally be conditioned by his own peculiar balance of instincts, sentiments and emotions. A creed (in the academic sense) may indeed prompt him to seek certain kinds of experiences which without it he might miss. But it is equally certain that the absence of such a creed does not preclude the possibility of the experiences in question. In any case, his interpretation of them will fall into terms of the intellectualistic theory of the universe which he happens to hold.

Until we grasp this elementary fact, we are shut out from any scientific or humane catholicity of appreciation of the world of religious experience — that strange and obscure chamber of reality whence come the airs from heaven and blasts from hell, the joys and terrors, the dumb despairs and the transfiguring inspirations, which have coloured the lives of some of the most remarkable figures in history. But when we understand and apply it rightly, we shall be able to classify together, and explain by the same scientific formula, the religious experiences of Catholic Saints such as Augustine, Francis of Assisi, Francis of Sales, Catherine of Siena, Teresa; mystics like Meister Eckhardt; Protestant visionaries like Bunyan, Wesley, and George Fox; freethinkers like Shelley and John Stuart Mill; and, last but not least, of the gifted poet whose tragic career and untimely death we are led to deplore anew by the publication of his Life, and of his collected works.[1]

The common natural elements in all these cases, and indeed in any possible case of religious re-birth, could not be more concisely described than by Professor James, in the concluding chapter of the work to which we have already referred. He sets forth the process of conversion as follows: —

It consists of two parts: —

(1) An uneasiness; and
(2) Its solution.

(1) The uneasiness, reduced to its simplest terms, is a sense that there is *something wrong about us* as we naturally stand.

(2) The solution is a sense that *we are saved from the wrongness* by making proper connection with the higher powers.

In those more developed minds which alone we are studying, the wrongness takes a moral character, and the salvation takes a mystical tinge. I think we shall keep well within the limits of what is common to all

[1] *The Life of Francis Thompson*, by Everard Meynell. *The Works of Francis Thompson*. Edited by Wilfrid Meynell. In three volumes. (London: Burns & Oates, 1913.)

such minds if we formulate the essence of their religious
experience in terms like these: —

The individual, so far as he suffers from his wrongness
and criticises it, is to that extent consciously beyond it,
and in at least possible touch with something higher, if
anything higher exist. Along with the wrong part there
is thus a better part of him, even though it may be but
a most helpless germ. With which part he should identify his real being is by no means obvious at this stage;
but when stage 2 (the stage of solution or salvation)
arrives, the man identifies his real being with the germi-
nal higher part of himself; and does so in the following
way. *He becomes conscious that this higher part is conterminous and continuous with a* MORE *of the same quality, which is operative in the universe outside of him, and
which he can keep in working touch with, and in a fashion
get on board of and save himself when all his lower being
has gone to pieces in the wreck.*[1]

The question how a man, passing through such an
experience, shall interpret it, depends naturally, as we
have said, on his philosophic outlook, or on the theological creed he holds. The scientific student, however,
is bound to discriminate closely between the actual
data and the theoretic elements in the subject's own
account of his case. The business of science is neither
to accept at its face value the theological or philosophical explanation, nor yet to deny the reality of the
facts explained. The modern freethinker who declares
that there is "nothing in it" — that conversion is a
mere fiction or figment of the imagination — is as

---

[1] *The Varieties of Religious Experience*, p. 508.

widely astray as the primitive believer who imagines that every article of his creed is verified by the transition which he is conscious of having undergone. It is very necessary to hold fast, as a clue to the labyrinth of religious and psychic experiences, to the almost platitudinous remark of Fechner: "Nichts wirkliches kann unmöglich sein." It is also indispensable to remember that between, let us say, John Stuart Mill and St. Augustine, or between Shelley and Francis Thompson, there is no difference of nature, however wide may be the gulf between their theories. Thompson himself has well said that in modern poetry, "what is great and good for the non-Catholic is for the most part great and good for the Catholic." He need not have qualified the statement, and he might well have added that what is actually true for the one is true for the other.

It is inevitable that a man of stunted or starved emotional nature and rationalistic mental tendencies, who has undergone conversion, will give a prosaic account of his experience, which, nevertheless, the dispassionate student will find sufficiently startling and interesting. Indeed, such a man's story may turn out to be, from the psychological point of view, all the more useful and informing because he keeps close to the ground of literal fact. This is what we find in the account which Mill gives in his "Autobiography" of his own transition from despair to moral reassurance and the sense of purpose and meaning in life. As this remarkable book is much less read than it deserves to be, and as many readers might fail to realize that the account in chapter v of "A Crisis in My Mental History" is just as truly the story of a religious conversion as St. Augustine's picture of what happened to him in the garden, I shall venture to quote it at some length: —

> From the winter of 1821, when I first read Bentham, and especially from the commencement of the *Westminster Review*, I had what might truly be called an object in life; to be a reformer of the world. My conception of my own happiness was entirely identified with this object. The personal sympathies I wished for were those of fellow labourers in this enterprise. . . .
>
> This did very well for several years, during which the general improvement going on in the world and the idea of myself as engaged with others in struggling to promote it, seemed enough to fill up an interesting and animated existence. But the time came when I awakened from this as from a dream. It was in the autumn of 1826.[1] I was in a dull state of nerves, such as everybody is occasionally liable to; unsusceptible to enjoyment or pleasurable excitement; one of those moods when what is pleasure at other times, becomes insipid or indifferent; *the state, I should think, in which converts to Methodism usually are, when smitten by their first "conviction of sin."* [2] In this frame of mind it occurred to me to put the question directly to myself: "Suppose that all your objects in life were realized; that all the changes in institutions and opinions which you are looking forward to, could be completely effected at this very instant; would this be a great joy and happiness to you?" And an irrepressible

---

[1] He was then twenty years old — a fact which the student of religious psychology will note with interest.

[2] Italics the present writer's.

self-consciousness distinctly answered, "No." At this
my heart sank within me; the whole foundation on which
my life was constructed fell down. All my happiness was
to have been found in the continual pursuit of this end.
The end had ceased to charm, and how could there ever
again be any interest in the means? I seemed to have
nothing left to live for.

At first I hoped that the cloud would pass away of
itself; but it did not. A night's sleep, the sovereign rem-
edy for the smaller vexations of life, had no effect on it.
I awoke to a renewed consciousness of the woeful fact.
I carried it with me into all companies, into all occupa-
tions. Hardly anything had power to cause me even a
few minutes' oblivion of it. For some months the cloud
seemed to grow thicker and thicker. The lines in Coleridge's "Dejection" — I was not then acquainted with
them — exactly describe my case: —

> A grief without a pang, void, dark and drear,
> A drowsy, stifled, unimpassioned grief,
> Which finds no natural outlet or relief
> In word, or sigh, or tear.

In vain I sought relief from my favourite books;
those memorials of past nobleness and greatness from
which I had always hitherto drawn strength and ani-
mation. I read them now without feeling, or with the
accustomed feeling *minus* all its charm; and I became
persuaded, that my love of mankind, and of excellence
for its own sake, had worn itself out. . . .

I was thus, as I said to myself, left stranded at the
commencement of my voyage, with a well-equipped ship
and a rudder, but no sail; without any real desire for the
ends which I had been so carefully fitted out to work for;
no delight in virtue, or the general good, but also just as

little in anything else. The fountains of vanity and am-
bition seemed to have dried up within me, as completely
as those of benevolence. . . .

These were the thoughts which mingled with the dry,
heavy dejection of the melancholy winter of 1826–27.
During this time I was not incapable of my usual occu-
pations. I went on with them mechanically, by the mere
force of habit. . . . Two lines of Coleridge, in whom
alone of all writers I have found a true description of
what I felt, were often in my thoughts, not at this time
(for I had never read them), but in a later period of the
same mental malady: —

> Work without hope draws nectar in a sieve,
> And hope without an object cannot live.

In all probability my case was by no means so peculiar
as I fancied it, and I doubt not that many others have
passed through a similar state; but the idiosyncrasies of
my education had given to the general phenomenon a
special character, which made it seem the natural effect
of causes that it was hardly possible for time to remove.
*I frequently asked myself, if I could, or if I was bound to go
on living when life must be passed in this manner. I generally answered to myself that I did not think I could possibly
bear it beyond a year.*[1] When, however, not more than
half that duration of time had elapsed, a small ray of
light broke in upon my gloom. I was reading, accidentally, Marmontel's "Mémoires," and came to the passage
which relates his father's death, the distressed position of
the family, and the sudden inspiration by which he, then
a mere boy, felt and made them feel that he would be
everything to them — would supply the place of all
that they had lost. A vivid conception of the scene and

[1] Italics mine.

its feelings came over me, and I was moved to tears. From this moment my burden grew lighter. The oppression of the thought that all feeling was dead within me was gone. I was no longer hopeless: I was not a stock or a stone. I had still, it seemed, some of the material out of which all worth of character, and all capacity for happiness, are made. Relieved from my ever-present sense of irremediable wretchedness, I gradually found that the ordinary incidents of life could again give me some pleasure; that I could again find enjoyment, not intense, but sufficient for cheerfulness, in sunshine and sky, in books, in conversation, in public affairs; and that there was, once more, excitement, though of a moderate kind, in exerting myself for my opinions, and for the public good. Thus the cloud gradually drew off, and I again enjoyed life; and though I had several relapses, some of which lasted many months, I never again was as miserable as I had been.

Let any student of psychology compare this in detail with the story of St. Augustine, or with Francis Thompson's "Hound of Heaven," and the conclusion will present itself to his mind with irresistible force that all three men are talking about the same thing. They have trodden the same paths, and the reality with which they have come into redeeming contact is the same in each case. Each has discovered that the good in himself is, in James's words, "conterminous and continuous with a *more* of the same quality, which is operative in the universe outside of him, and which he can . . . in a fashion get on board of and save himself when all his lower being has gone to pieces in the wreck."

Let us turn first to the relevant passage in the "Confessions" of St. Augustine. After he has left Alypius, when he is weeping and groaning in spirit, he hears the heavenly voice commanding, "Tolle, lege; Tolle, lege." He returns to Alypius, takes the scroll of the Apostle, opens it at random, and reads the text on which his eye first falls: "Non in comessationibus et ebrietatibus, non in cubilibus et impudicitiis, non in contentione et aemulatione; sed induite Dominum Jesum Christum, et carnis providentiam ne feceritis in concupiscentiis." [1] Returning in sudden marvellous tranquillity to Alypius, Augustine shows him what he has read, and Alypius immediately points out, and applies to himself, the words that follow: "Him that is weak in the faith receive ye."

No student can fail to note the comparative triviality of the texts which, cropping up at the critical moment, effected the change both in Mill and St. Augustine. The latter, prompted, as he tells us, by an inner voice, opens the Epistle to the Romans at random, and reads a text with which he must have been long familiar; Mill declares that he was reading Marmontel "by chance." One cannot but feel that any one of a thousand other passages of literature, met with at the appropriate moment, would have produced the same effect; for that effect is the natural supervention of

[1] Romans XIII, 13 and 14, R.V.: "Not in revelling and drunkenness, not in chambering and wantonness, not in strife and jealousy. But put ye on the Lord Jesus Christ, and make not provision for the flesh, to fulfil the lusts thereof."

calm after storm. Nowhere in all literature is there so wonderful an account of a protracted period of spiritual struggle as is contained in the chapters of St. Augustine's "Confessions," preceding the incident in the garden. While Mill enters into no such minute introspective analysis, he nevertheless lets us see that his depression had lasted for at least half a year, and that it was so serious that he frequently asked himself whether he could even continue to live, if life must be passed in this manner, and had come to the conclusion that he could not endure it beyond a year. In his anxiety not to exaggerate, moreover, he even falls into self-contradiction by minimizing the greatness of his salvation. He tells us in one sentence that it was only "a *small* ray of light" that broke upon his gloom. Yet the next few sentences, though written many years after the event, and with evident self-restraint, break into an emotional enthusiasm very rare with the analytic logician and economist, and amount to an assertion that he passed from death unto life. Truly an amazing effect to be produced by "a small ray of light"!

We cannot, in any ultimate sense, *explain* these mysterious moods of the soul. We can only say, in the words of the "Imitation," "Left to ourselves we sink and perish; visited we lift up our heads and live." Our inability to explain the matter, however, is no deeper here than in any other case of natural phenomena. No scientific explanation really explains anything; at best, it tells us of uniformity in sequence, and enables us to anticipate a given phenomenon when we encounter its customary antecedent. The psychic turmoil of religious experience is just as explicable, and just as inexplicable, as the transition of the sea from storm to calm. Between the facts of outward nature there is no logical, no rational nexus. We know *that* they happen; experience shows us the *order* in which they happen; but *why* they happen remains a mystery — or an idle question. They are never logically deducible from each other, as are the facts of geometry from the principles of mathematics. Yet this in no wise invalidates our scientific generalizations, and renders them no whit less useful than they would be if the phenomena followed logically from one another.

We must not, therefore, allow the supernaturalists and miracle-mongers to hoodwink us into believing that there is anything more marvellous in religious conversion than there is in the growth of flowers or the sequence of the seasons. If — or rather when — we become able to state and control the conditions under which religious experience always occurs, we shall have as complete a scientific mastery of it as we have of agriculture or mineralogy.

We have compared two stories of conversion, one that of an ancient Catholic, the other that of a modern freethinker, and found their identity in all essential details. We have seen that the data are the same in both cases, and that only the theoretical explanation differs. Or rather, it would be more accurate to say that the Catholic saint offers a theoretical explanation, in the shape of his theology, whereas the freethinker is content to state the facts without attempting any interpretation. Lest our parallel seem inadequate, as applying to two individuals both remarkable rather for philosophic and psychological insight than for poetic imagination, let us turn to the case of two poets, as far apart in their theological doctrines as Augustine and Mill, yet both unconsciously testifying to the same kind of experience. Even Professor James never discovered the fact that Shelley underwent a conversion. Yet any student of religious psychology who will read successively Shelley's "Hymn to Intellectual Beauty" and Francis Thompson's "Hound of Heaven," will have the same overwhelming sense of identity between the experiences testified to, as arises from comparing the cases of Augustine and Mill, or indeed any two stories of conversion within the limits of the Christian *Weltanschauung*. Thompson, it is true, depicts himself as fleeing from the celestial pursuer; Shelley apparently embraces it on the first challenge. After telling at some length of the "unseen Power" whose awful shadow "floats though unseen amongst us, — visiting this various world with as inconstant wing as summer winds that creep from flower to flower," he proceeds to relate how, —

> Musing deeply on the lot
> Of life, at the sweet time when winds are wooing

> All vital things that wake to bring
> News of birds and blossoming,
> Sudden thy shadow fell on me:
> I shrieked, and clasped my hands in ecstasy!

He tells how he dedicated his life to the unseen Power, and calls the universe to testify that he has kept his vow. He claims that, after this one decisive moment of insight and quickening, —

> . . . never joy illumed my brow
> Unlinked with hope that thou wouldst free
> This world from its dark slavery;
> That thou, O awful Loveliness,
> Wouldst give whate'er these words cannot express.

That the effects of Shelley's conversion upon his conduct may not always have been such as we can conscientiously approve, in no way weakens my contention. It is notorious that under every religious discipline these effects are often unsatisfactory. Even in the case of Thompson, after the "following feet" have overtaken him, and he has discovered that his gloom was, after all, "shade of His hand, outstretched caressingly," there were many incidents which caused distress to his friends, and pangs of conscience to himself. Yet nobody can doubt that the tone and level of life for both these men were permanently changed by the mystical experiences which they so wonderfully record. Shelley at the last, in his "Ode to the West Wind," implicitly renews the proud claim that he has not been disobedient unto the heavenly vision. He speaks not only as a poet, but as a prophet, who indeed feels himself despised and rejected, and yet is in no wise uncertain as to the authenticity of his prophetic credentials. He still believes that his "dead thoughts," driven over the universe, would have power "to quicken a new birth." Hope may be extinct, but faith is not. As much as Thompson, he had come into vivifying touch with a real Power of goodness, outside himself but continuous with the good in him.

This, then, is the position which an examination of cases of conversion justifies us in assuming: that the experience of all the converts is identical, and that the Power-not-themselves, which enters into and transfigures their life, is always the same Power. Nor is the holding of any special form of theological creed, or indeed of any creed at all, a necessary condition for experiencing this quickening contact. Whether the convert calls the power that saves him "The Spirit of Intellectual Beauty," or "Christ living in me," or the "Fugitive Ideal," or "The Hound of Heaven," we know that what is connoted is always the same factor in experience. We know this scientifically, just as we know any other fact of nature. Science has no other criterion for discovering the identity of an energy manifested in different times and places, except the twin facts that it always appears under the same conditions and always produces the same effects.

It may be granted that our psychological investigation reveals the identity of the saving factor which enters into the lives of men of all creeds and of none;

yet the significance of this fact may be overlooked by
those who are accustomed to thinking only in the conventional theological terms. Such thinkers may not
realize that the admission of the simple psychological
fact, if fact it be, which we have thus defined, annihil-
ates for ever the pretension that any supernaturalistic
doctrine — Catholic, "Episcopalian," Methodist or
any other — is necessary to salvation. If men like
Mill and Shelley, whom the orthodox world would
unhesitatingly rank as atheists, can be shown to have
undergone exactly the same experience as St. Augustine or St. Paul, and the experience in their case led to
results analogous to those wrought in the lives of the
great Christian saints, it becomes self-evident that the
doctrinal machinery for bringing the individual soul
into contact with the redeeming power is in no wise indispensable. This conclusion may be unwelcome to the
dogmatist, but it will be hailed with joy by all who feel
not only that the world is passing away from the orthodox postulates, but that, by every canon of intellectual
integrity, it ought to do so. The ecclesiastical conditions of salvation are for many of us intellectually and
morally impossible ones. We cannot believe to order,
and we cannot believe either in the absence of historical
evidence or in defiance of such evidence as we have.
If a man of modern education cannot undergo conversion except he believe in the physical resurrection
of Jesus Christ, or in the continued self-conscious existence of the individualized personality of Jesus Christ

after death, then conversion is impossible for him; he is, as we said at the outset, excluded from an infinitely precious and exalting experience. If, on the other hand, we can show actual cases of men who, holding no such beliefs, have yet entered into this saving experience, we have conclusively demonstrated the superfluousness of the ecclesiastical doctrine.

The principle that "Nothing real can be impossible" is thus seen to be a two-edged sword. It forces us to admit the reality of many abnormal experiences under the Christian theory which the iconoclastic free-thinker is disposed to reject with contemptuous incredulity. On the other hand, it compels the Christian dogmatist to concede that his dogma is no condition *sine quâ non* for the occurrence of such experiences.

A careful investigation, conducted with all the rigorous precautions of scientific psychology, will, we believe, demonstrate that religious experience of the kind of which St. Paul and St. Augustine are classic instances, is much less rare than we commonly imagine it to be. If the factors involved are natural and normal in human experience, it seems probable that many people will pass through just such transformations, though, owing to their unawareness of the kinship of their own cases with those of the great spiritual geniuses, they may never say or even know that they have experienced conversion. Yet the essential facts are quite plainly universal facts. We are, in simple truth, all dependent, as Matthew Arnold points out, on a Power greater than ourselves, yet identical and continuous with the highest element of our selfhood. We do not make ourselves, our nature or our circumstances. We cannot explain or control the fact that a bodily ailment which on one day is an overwhelming obstacle to any great achievement, is, on another day, a most potent incentive to the attainment of our possible highest. Energies and inspirations, "facilities and felicities," do indeed seem to come and go independently of our volition. "Unless above himself he can erect himself, how poor a thing is man!" This undeniably applies not only to the rare spiritual genius, but to what James calls "the Crumps and Stigginses."

Equally universal is the experience of what St. Paul calls "the war in our members." A man may be altogether irreligious, he may be entirely self-centred; yet even he will be sometimes able and sometimes unable to do what seems to him good. His ideal may be an idol, his notion of good may be sordid, yet he will experience a kind of rhythmic alternation in his power to approximate towards it. And in proportion as a man's notions of duty are more exalted, in that proportion the conflict between aspiration and achievement becomes more apparent and more unendurable. The saint who cries out, "Oh, wretched man that I am, who shall deliver me from the body of this death?" is giving utterance to a feeling that occurs to every man and woman. Or, if we are forced to admit that this experience is not quite universal, we shall at once see that the absence of it in particular individuals is the decisive measure of their spiritual poverty and shallowness. He who does not know what it is to miss the mark morally, he who has no aspirations that transcend his capacity of achievement, and who never finds the wail of St. Paul echoing in his own heart, is spiritually deficient to such an extent that he is almost below the human level. He stands to morality as a blind man to colour or a deaf man to music. Nay, he is even worse off than these, for these are at least aware that there is a realm of human experience from which they are excluded, and they do undoubtedly lament the bitter misfortune which shuts them out from it. The man who is morally blind and deaf is unconscious of his condition. He sneers at the alleged experience of others, and denies the reality of the ideals which men strive in vain to attain. He has not even risen so high as to feel "the desire of the moth for the star, of the night for the morrow."

The experience of moral inability, however, is scarcely more universal in human consciousness than the experience of the influx of moral power. Who is there that upon challenge must not admit that he has often been helped, as it were by a Power outside himself, towards the fulfilment of his ethical aspirations? Who has not known at least some rare moments when the ideal flooded the spirit with strength and joy? And the strength and joy that come are almost invariably in inverse ratio to the intensity and bitterness of the struggle which has preceded their arrival.

Yet this experience, so ordinary that most men never dream of classifying it as religious, is essentially identical with the most wonderful instances of conversion which literature records. Not being poets, we may not, with Shelley, "shriek and clasp our hands in ecstasy" when the awful Loveliness reaches the volitional springs of our nature. We may not envisage the challenging ideals that rebuke us as the hunting of the soul by the Hound of Heaven. And, not being analytical psychologists, we may not, with John Stuart Mill, realize that our gloom and depression are identical with the Methodist's conviction of sin, and our deliverance from them one and the same with the Methodist's new birth. Yet reflection and scientific comparison of cases make the fact of this identity altogether undeniable.

But what is the Power that saves? What is this thing of many names, whose every title is so obviously inadequate? It is the Hound of Heaven; it is the Spirit of Intellectual Beauty; it is the voice that calls to St. Augustine, "Tolle, lege; tolle, lege." Yet such imaginative characterizations are clearly not definite enough for purposes of scientific classification. And from this point of view, to call the saving power "God" is no more helpful than to call it x, unless we have succeeded in evaluating x, or, in other words, in defining God in terms of verifiable experience.

Our analysis, however, opens up to us the way by which such an evaluation may be reached. If we attend closely to what happens in the case of those who experience conversion, we find that what they mean by God is, in the first place, the source of the supreme blessings of life. Not only so, but we find that this ultimate source of moral strength and spiritual peace and joy is a natural as distinct from a supernatural, an empirical as distinct from a transcendental, power. In every case, from St. Paul and St. Augustine to Shelley and John Stuart Mill, what happens is clearly the unlocking of the hitherto unexploited resources of the man's own selfhood, by a key obtained from *some other human agency*. There is no instance of conversion unmediated by social influences. Even if a man sees a heavenly vision, as did St. Paul, it is always the vision of a human form; and the context of circumstance always demonstrates that the efficient cause of the experience is the stored-up memory of what that human form stood for when it was alive under the limitations of earthly experience, and not something which it has done since its withdrawal from within the spiritual organism of living human society. When the transformation is effected through the reading of a sentence in a book, the humanness of the source of salvation is still more evident. The command to abandon self-indulgence and to "put on the Lord Jesus Christ" originated not in a transcendental sphere, but in the thought of the man Paul. Nobody has ever claimed that Marmontel's "Mémoires" were either dictated or inspired by any superhuman power. Nor would the most hidebound dogmatist dream of supposing that there does actually and objectively exist a Hound of Heaven, which pursues a man as the dogs pursue the fox. Thompson's Hound and Shelley's Spirit of Intellectual Beauty are quite obviously objectifications, poetic bodyings forth, of a mighty ideal which haunts their minds. And this ideal is not a thing which they have created by their own unaided reflection. However great may be their own original contribution, they have received from others — from parents and teachers, and from the living tradition which, through literature, gives a timeless life to human thought and aspiration — the materials out of which they have constructed their imaginative picture of the ideal that haunts them and will not let them go.

It is necessary to emphasize the fact that a psychological investigation of religious experience definitely disproves the hideous Calvinistic (or more truly Augustinian) doctrine of total depravity. If man were totally depraved, he would necessarily remain for ever ignorant of the fact, just as a community of men born blind would remain unaware of the existence of vision. Unless there is something in a man's own nature identical with the goodness that is outside of him, he could never come into contact with the larger forces of spiritual strength; for he could never recognize goodness as such. This truth has been stated once for all by Im-

manuel Kant in his treatise on "The Metaphysic of
Ethics": "Even the Holy One in the Gospel," says
Kant, "is only recognized to be so when compared with
our *ideal* of moral excellence. . . . Whence this idea
God, as the supreme archetypal good? Simply from
that idea of ethical perfection evolved by reason *a
priori*. . . . Imitation has no place in morals."

Into the metaphysical question whether the native-
born good in man is "evolved by reason *a priori*" we
need not here enter. It suffices for our purpose that
there is an original goodness in man, whatever may
be its genesis. It is in virtue of this endowment of our
nature that we recognize goodness as such, whether we
find it incarnated in a living being, or objectified in the
concept of a superhuman person. It is also in virtue
of the fact that goodness is the fundamental element
of our nature that we realize the inexhaustibility of the
ethical ideal. We see that no one man can ever embody
to the full the entire possibility of goodness. This is as
true of Christ as of any other historic personage. Deep
and real as our sense of his unsurpassed greatness may
be, we cannot for a moment regard him as more than
one illustration, one hint, of the possibilities of moral
realization. We may say of him in his relation to the
universal ideal, as Mr. William Watson says of the
sun in its relation to the personified totality of the
physical world: —

> Thou art but as a word of his speech;
> Thou art but as a wave of his hand;

Thou art brief as a glitter of sand
'Twixt tide and tide on his beach;
Thou art less than a spark of his fire,
Or a moment's mood of his soul;
Thou art lost in the notes on the lips of his choir
That chant the chant of the Whole.

Nor should it be imagined that when we speak of
God as the Ideal we are in any way invalidating or denying the reality of God. There could not be a grosser
blunder, nor one more disastrous in its consequences,
than the antithesis between the ideal and the real.
People talk as though the real were coextensive only
with the actual, the visible and tangible, and as though
anything which does not possess these attributes were
unreal. But if — without going into metaphysical considerations — we take the merely empirical ground that
whatever produces effects is real, and that the most
real thing is that which produces the most powerful effects, we see at once that ideals are more and not less
real than the phenomena of the sense-world. Only
that is unreal which does nothing and can do nothing.
Yet nobody, not even the most thoroughgoing materialist, can deny that ideals do produce astonishingly
great and tangible effects in the lives of individuals, and
of human society in mass. It may indeed be maintained
that the ideal is itself a mere projection in consciousness of material things previously experienced through
sensation. That is a tenable position, — impossible as
it may be for the materialist to explain how physical
facts can translate themselves into facts of conscious-

ness and standards of moral valuation. Yet even this explanation by the materialist will leave untouched the fact for which alone I am concerned at the moment to contend — that the ideal as such, whatever its genesis, is an actual potency, a cause, a force acting upon the mind and will of man, and through these producing effects more significant than any merely physical process could ever achieve.

To say, then, that God is the Ideal or that the Ideal is God, is equivalent to saying that God is the supreme Reality. It is also equivalent to identifying God with the human and natural; for few would be disposed to contend that an ideal which is our deepest nature can be at the same time supernatural in the sense of super-human. Super-individual it undeniably is. Often, too, it is higher or deeper than consciousness, even in a man of whose conduct it is the regulative principle, dominant over all special passions and all merely self-centred striving. But super-social it is not; at least, we have no experience which could verify the assertion that it is. Nor need we be concerned either to prove or disprove its transcendence in this sense. Its value to man, its preciousness and power, are wholly inherent in that aspect of it which is within the realm of verifiable experience. Even, therefore, if it could be shown to be coextensive not merely with human rationality but with inconceivable choirs and hierarchies of spiritual self-consciousness beyond time and space, and independent of the limitations that condition our mortality, it could acquire from that consideration no dignity, no majesty, no sanctity beyond what attaches to its humblest manifestation as the energizing principle of good in the poorest and least intellectual human being.

The view of God which I am here attempting to outline, based as it is on ethical psychology, and built up out of demonstrable elements of experience, is a view which makes atheism impossible. Or, more precisely — since the term atheism denotes a volitional rather than an intellectual attitude — I should say that it renders impossible the denial of the existence of God. Only on two grounds could anybody base a negative argument against this doctrine. He might say that no such comprehensive inter-personal and super-personal ideal exists; but this contention we have refuted in advance, by pointing to effects which presuppose such an ideal as their cause. Or he might contend that, inasmuch as this ideal is built up out of volitions, sentiments, likes and dislikes, and not out of purely rational judgments, it ought not to command the allegiance of a creature like man, in whom reason is the distinctive and highest faculty. Here again, however, our answer is not far to seek. We need only point to the fact, elementary in ethical philosophy, that the discursive reason of man has no place whatever in determining the values and the ends of life. The reason is at home only in the realm of fact. It is the will which is sovereign in the sphere of values. Our moral judgments are ultimate facts, which the reason may classify and systematize, but which it can neither validate nor invalidate.[1] A creature all intellect, but devoid of those instincts, sentiments and emotions out of which concrete moral judgments are built up, could never come to feel the constraining force of any moral ideal, whether apprehended as purely abstract, or objectified in any one personal incarnation. But man, happily, is not thus constituted. He does spontaneously love goodness when it is set before him. He is rebuked from within himself by the clash between what he does and what he ought to do. The "ought" of conscience is irreducible. The reality of the ideal is proved not so much by a man's conduct as by his own dissatisfaction with it. Francis Thompson is actually pursued by the Hound of Heaven, and he is never more conscious of the pursuer than when he is apparently remotest from it.

The special temptations to which Thompson was subjected, raise anew the old hard problem as to which type of character is of greater moral worth — the man to whom goodness comes easily, who does the work of the stern Lawgiver and knows it not, who is not embarrassed or deflected from the right path by the solicitations of the senses; or he who achieves good-

[1] That is, as facts of consciousness. It is not intended to deny that conscience is rational, that moral distinctions relate to objective differences, and that the promotion of "the good of all" is a commandment of reason. The contention is merely that the ethical facts could not enter into a consciousness which was devoid of will. The perception of good and evil as such springs out of the clash between what is and what is desired.

ness, if at all, only at the cost of a long and bitter struggle. It sounds paradoxical to say that a man who only abstains, let us say, from drunkenness by means of severe and heroic effort is a better man than he who never feels any inclination to drink to excess. Yet it is still more paradoxical to attribute a higher degree of virtue to him who has never known temptation than to him who has fought the enemy at its strongest and fiercest, and come out victorious, even though not unscathed.

The problem does not arise in the case of the un-tempted man who is self-satisfied. The most repellent creature under heaven is the moral prig. The rich man who never stole, the strong man who never drank, the man of ascetic temperament who never felt the call of the flesh — these, if they thank God that in such matters they are not as other men, are nearer to hell than the man who is heart-broken at his own badness and weakness. Nor is there any question in the case of the much-tempted man who after many battles has at last found peace in self-conquest. For he, having suffered much, has learned a sympathy with human-ity and an insight into the moral needs of others which fit him to be a guide and counsellor to those in trial, as the untried man can never be.

These considerations are relevant when we think of the tragic element in Thompson's life, represented by his battle with the fiend laudanum. Having been indiscreetly presented by his mother with a copy of

De Quincey's "Confessions of an English Opium-Eater," the unhappy youth, who had been forced into a study of medicine which was repellent to him, took refuge from the realities of Manchester — and later of the London underworld — in the dreamland of that soul-destroying drug. Of men so tempted as Coleridge, De Quincey and Thompson, we should think with an infinite sympathy, thanking God not that we are not as they but that we have never been tried as they. Given their temptations, we might have proved as far inferior to them in moral courage and strength as in poetic genius. And nobody who reads Thompson's prose and poetry can fail to see how every temptation and every suffering has been transmuted by him into wisdom and literary beauty.

My present purpose constrains me to subdue the controversial impulse awakened by the staggering assertion of a recent English critic, that the author of the "Anthem of Earth," the "Ode to the Setting Sun," and "The Hound of Heaven," was not a great poet. I find it equally hard to resist the temptation to dilate at length on the wonderful qualities of Thompson's prose. The study of his essays encourages a man to deny what the world at large accepts as a self-evident fact — namely, that all human speech is divided into prose and poetry, and therefore that whatever is not poetry is prose. Even M. Bergson, despite the rarity of such a literary style as his own, acquiesces in this vulgar error. When that amusing philistine, the

Bourgeois Gentilhomme of Molière, is told that such sentences as "Nicole, apportez-moi mes pantoufles" are prose, he expresses huge delight: "Par ma foi, il y a plus de quarante ans que je dis de la prose, sans que j'en susse rien; et je vous suis le plus obligé du monde de m'avoir appris cela!" Everybody laughs at his simplicity; yet perhaps they who laugh are simpler than he. At all events, one who has learned to know intimately and to love those supreme prose styles which are perhaps a more distinctive glory of our English speech than even its poetic miracles, will feel disposed to contend hotly, as I do, that not all speech which is not poetry is worthy to be called prose. If the "Areopagitica" of Milton, the first book of Hooker's "Ecclesiastical Polity," the "Religio Medici" and "Urn Burial" of Sir Thomas Browne, and certain quintessential things in Jeremy Taylor, Edmund Burke, Ruskin, Walter Pater and Francis Thompson are prose, — as indeed they are, — then we deny that the thing which masquerades as English in the columns of our daily newspapers and constitutes the poverty-stricken vocabulary of current speech, is worthy to be dignified by the same title. It is no more prose than the verse of Miss Wells's delightful "Whimsey Anthology" is poetry. M. Jourdain was right, even though only instinctively so. He felt the gulf between his talk and the French of Montaigne, of Pascal, of St. François de Sales. Daily speech — the language of the newspaper and the market-place —

is at best only crude ore. It has to be crushed and sifted, and treated in a hundred ways, before the refined gold which is prose can be extracted from it; and then, out of that refined gold, are cast or moulded or beaten the ornaments and medallions which are poetry.

There is much, indeed, which hovers on the border-line between real prose and counterfeit. Many times one may be in doubt as to the classification of what one is reading. But whoever has once felt the wizard spell of our "God-gifted organ-voices" will never again be in doubt when the authentic oracle speaks. It is not necessary for such an one to read more than a single page of Thompson's "Paganism, Old and New," or of his essay on Shelley, to realize that here is a new incarnation of the ancient genius of English speech. When one first dips into his pages, the sensation is unmistakable. One feels

> like some watcher of the skies
> When a new planet swims into his ken!

Thompson's rebuke to the authorities of his Church, in the second paragraph of the Shelley essay, is alone sufficient to settle the question once for all: —

Fathers of the Church (we would say), pastors of the Church, pious laics of the Church: you are taking from its walls the panoply of Aquinas; take also from its walls the psaltery of Alighieri. Unrol the precedents of the Church's past; recall to your minds that Francis of Assisi was among the precursors of Dante; that, sworn

to Poverty, he forswore not Beauty, but discerned
through the lamp Beauty the Light God. . . .

Truly may we say, the distinction between prose and
sub-prose is immensely clearer than that between
prose and poetry. Nay, rather, of the two distinctions
we should be more inclined to deny the existence of the
second. For prose is often only poetry at her ease.
Take this exquisite phrase of Thompson's, that Francis of Assisi "discerned through the lamp Beauty the
Light God." There is far less poetry in many a score
of lines, even by authentic singers, than in that one
perfect gem of prose. Nor need one quote the prose-
poem which comes a few pages later, beginning "The
universe is his box of toys," since all true lovers of the
supreme in letters either have it by heart or will prefer to read it in its own context. 52016

It is one of the bitter ironies of life that even in the
case of a predestinate poet like Thompson, his sweetest music can only be wrung from him by sorrow. There
is no fact which constitutes a more unanswerable argument for those who doubt or deny the almightiness of
God. The fact is undeniable: Suffering of some sort,
mental or physical, is the indispensable condition of
supreme achievement. Milton's anguish over his blindness carries him up to two of the highest of his Hima-
layan peaks of song — the sonnet on his blindness, and
the invocation to the Holy Light which opens the third
Book of "Paradise Lost." Nor can it be doubted that
the insight of Thompson into the deeps of human woe

has been sharpened, and his utterance rendered more poignant and memorable, by his own descent into that London which is much like hell. The glorious outcome of the process, however, can never furnish a moral justification for it.

> Half a beast is the great god Pan,
> To laugh as he sits by the river
>   Making a poet out of a man;
>   The true gods sigh for the cost and the pain —
>   For the reed which grows nevermore again
> As a reed with the reeds in the river!

Mr. Wilfrid Meynell has disclosed the interesting fact that the "Shelley" and "The Hound of Heaven" were " contemporaries — one could say twins." They belong to the days when their author was recovering from the deep wound of his outcast period, and fighting his bitter battle with the drug-fiend and with the harpy melancholy which the struggle brought upon him. Francis Thompson, a failure for lack of vocation as a candidate for the priesthood, failing as a medical student, failing even to enlist as a common soldier, a nervous wreck and addicted to drugs, wrought these two masterpieces out of his experience as a derelict in the streets of London, when he sold matches, papers or shoestrings, slept in fourpenny doss-houses when he had the money, and passed the night on the Embankment, "between heaven and Charing Cross" (or perhaps we should say between Charing Cross and hell), when he had not. We cannot cease to marvel at the mystery of such achievement growing out of such circumstances, even when we realize that only after the reed has been torn from the river, and hacked and hewed by the great god Pan, can it yield up its hidden music.

No denial or qualification is possible to Mr. George Wyndham's dictum that the essay on Shelley is "the most important contribution to pure letters written in English during the last twenty years." It is bitter to reflect how much sooner the fame he merited might have come to Thompson if the "Dublin Review" could have taken its tiny stock of courage in both hands and printed that essay when it was first received, instead of rejecting it, and bringing it out only after its creator had passed beyond the need of human help. Yet perhaps when we remember the hideous official tyranny that reigns within the Church of Rome — the malignity that pursued the great, the immortal George Tyrrell beyond death to his very grave — we ought rather to admire the hardihood of Mr. Wilfrid Ward in publishing the "Shelley" at all than wonder at the timorousness of his predecessors.

We would add to Mr. Wyndham's assertion the further statement that the essay on Shelley is the best possible commentary on its contemporary "The Hound of Heaven," and that both together are as invaluable for their autobiographical significance as for their unique literary quality. Reading in and between the lines of both, we get perhaps closer to the central self-hood of Francis Thompson than any narrator of the facts of his life could take us. Mr. Everard Meynell is undoubtedly right in emphasizing the personal significance of all the poems, and of such things in the prose as the essay on "Darkest England" and the "Shelley." Consider, for example, how self-revealing is his analysis of Shelley's childlikeness: "To be childlike," he says, "is to know not as yet that you are under sentence of life, nor petition that it be commuted into death." And what other pen could have drawn such a picture of Thompson as he has incidentally given of himself in describing the lot of Mangan: —

> Outcast from home, health and hope, with a charred past and a bleared future, an anchorite without detachment, and self-cloistered without self-sufficingness, deposed from a world which he had not abdicated, pierced with thorns which formed no crown, a poet hopeless of the bays, and a martyr hopeless of the palm . . . an exile banned and proscribed even from the innocent arms of childhood . . . burning helpless at the stake of his unquenchable heart.

If anybody doubts that this is autobiography, let him compare that phrase about "an exile banned and proscribed even from the innocent arms of childhood" with the agonized yearning of the following lines from "The Hound of Heaven": —

> I sought no more that after which I strayed
>   In face of man or maid;
> But still within the little children's eyes
>   Seems something, something that replies.
> *They* at least are for me, surely for me.

I turned me to them very wistfully;
But just as their young eyes grew sudden fair
    With dawning answers there,
Their angel plucked them from me by the hair. . . .

I have said that the indispensableness of suffering
to supreme achievement is no justification of it if
considered as part of a world-plan. But religion to-day,
if I mistake not, is no longer concerned to demonstrate
(as ordinary theism needs must try to do) that whatever is is right. The true religious lesson is not that the
entire frame of things is ruled in wisdom and goodness,
but rather the clue which experience gives to the use
which we can make of suffering. It is not only the poet
whom the great god Pan hacks and hews. We all have
our Gethsemanes, but most of us bleed vainly, not giving back to mankind in character and counsel what
we have endured in suffering. Turn your sorrow into
song! Like the child who tied his harpstring across the
bushes, let us learn the secret by which we may wring
from the storm its music. Let us not waste our time
in devising idle arguments to explain the inexplicable,
or to whitewash a world which is once for all indifferent
to our heart-breakings; but let us transmute the heavy
discipline of suffering and bereavement, as the poets
have always done, into some grace of character or gift
of work that shall help to redeem others. There is no
truer or wiser counsel for the sufferer than that given by
the quiet recluse to whom we owe the "Ecclesiastical
Music": —

If thou willingly bear thy cross, it will bear thee. . . .
If thou bear it unwillingly, thou makest thyself a burden
and greatly increasest thy load; and yet nevertheless
thou must bear it. If thou cast away one cross, without
doubt thou shalt find another, and perchance a heavier.

We have seen that the spiritual experience testified
to in "The Hound of Heaven" is possible to all men,
whether they be Catholic, Jew, Buddhist or Agnostic.
Let it suffice to add that that experience is also necessary to all men, if they are to have any elevation of
character, any spiritual dignity, any true valuation of
the finer ranges of existence. Our lives will be indeed
"strange, piteous, futile things" unless we too be
guided and goaded by the mighty Ideal which says to
us, as the celestial Hound to Thompson: "All things
betray thee who betrayest Me," "Nought shelters thee,
who wilt not shelter Me." Here speaks the voice of the
universal spiritual life which is our deepest selfhood,
and is therefore the secret of all worthy achievement,
of all art and poetry, of all reformation in the common
life. The spiritual barrenness of our day is due to our
indifference to it; and, in so far as we are overcoming
this barrenness, it is only in the measure in which we
are hearkening to the oracles of that voice, which can
always be heard by the attentive spirit. So indispensable to true humanity is this experience of the Ideal
that it were better for any man to be awakened to it
even by blinding sorrow than to remain all his days
at the level of sensuous self-centredness. To listen

within oneself for this voice is not to fall into the mean idolatry of self-deification, for when it speaks from within, it speaks always in condemnation of what we actually are. It is, nevertheless, our own voice — the Universal in the particular, the Man in men, the God in Man.

CHAPTER II

MR. G. K. CHESTERTON AS THEOLOGIAN

THERE is no more fascinating psychological problem in contemporary literature than that of the spiritual development of Mr. Gilbert Chesterton. His numerous books reveal him as a most perverse, yet a most lovable man. He belongs to a class, traceable in English letters from the days of Chaucer until now, which he has himself defined (in an essay on George Borrow) as that of the "character." He is a singular blend of the seemingly incompatible attributes of Sir John Falstaff and Dr. Samuel Johnson, combining the riotous good spirits of the one with much of the practical sagacity and moral sanity of the other.

One is struck, at the first glance over Mr. Chesterton's literary output, by his versatility. He has turned his hand to nearly every possible branch of the bookmaker's craft. During a comparatively short literary life, he has turned out poems, novels, biographical and critical studies, detective stories and — most singular of all — a Christian apologetic. Nearly two years ago, I ventured the assertion that the reason why he had not attempted the writing of plays was a well-grounded distrust of his own powers in that direction. I pointed out characteristics in his novels which

seemed to justify the conclusion that he could not
construct anything sufficiently close-knit and sequent
for dramatic presentation. Even a superficial study
of his numerous novels reveals a singular incoherence
in the workings of his fancy. In all his stories,
from "The Napoleon of Notting Hill," down to and
including "Manalive," one is impressed, and indeed
oppressed, by the chaotic looseness of the structure.
Characters appear and disappear, incident merges
into incident, with a reckless disregard of causality
and probability which makes them quite incapable of
reduction to dramatic form. Hence my conclusion
that he did not write plays because he could not.

Since then, Mr. Chesterton has very kindly gone to
the trouble (which must have been considerable) of
proving my point for me. It is no unkindness to say
of "Magic" that had it been written by any man
of less reputation it would never have got even into
print, let alone on to the stage. And, despite the attraction of its author's name and personality, and not-
withstanding all the help of an exquisite stage setting
and brilliant interpreters, it was such a failure (even
at the Little Theatre in London) that it would have
had to be taken off after a few performances, had not
Fleet Street come chivalrously to the rescue by working up a wholly artificial newspaper boom. Never was
such a set of mere masks put through such a series of
preposterous situations as in this "fantastic comedy."

Now, this fundamental incoherence, this recklessness of reality, is characteristic not only of Mr. Chesterton's creative fantasy, but also of his thought on the great issues of life and destiny. His mind is that of a spoiled child, and he spurns at logic as the spoiled child at parental authority. This inherent defect, moreover, has been intensified by the fact that, like almost all the successful literary men of the present day, he writes far too much. We find him every week in the "Illustrated London News" and the London "Daily Herald" (to which the allegiance lost by the "Daily News" has been transferred), and almost every month in almost every magazine. Nay, one cannot always open even that grave and reverend Roman quarterly, the "Dublin Review," nowadays, without finding Mr. Chesterton's motley jostling against the philosophic cloak of Mr. Wilfrid Ward. Now it would be inevitable, even with the most painstaking of craftsmen, that in such an output quality should be sacrificed to quantity; much more, then, with Mr. Chesterton, who is the least painstaking. Even his best and most finished work — even the ostensibly mature and considered judgments of "Heretics" and "Orthodoxy"— are palpably spoiled by haste. And no doubt the inadequacy of his book on Mr. Bernard Shaw is partly to be explained through the necessity of complying with time-conditions arbitrarily imposed by a commercial-minded publisher. In the latter essay, as its victim has pointed out, a whole chapter is spoiled, and the entire estimate of one of Mr.

Shaw's most important plays is reduced to absurdity, by a "howling misquotation."

This light-heartedness, this irresponsibility, which leads Mr. Chesterton, in an essay which he must have revised carefully for the press, to misquote and misrepresent an old and admired friend, will naturally play havoc with his judgments upon men and things towards which he stands in an attitude, not of sympathy, but of infuriated contempt. It is not too much to say that the tendency towards slipshod quotation and scorn for fact which seems native to him, and which has been developed by the habit of hasty work, has hardened into something like absolute incapacity to estimate fairly, or to express accurately, any point of view with which he does not agree. Take, for example, the following attempt on his part to make out that Ethical Societies and other liberal churches are exclusively composed of futile idiots, lectured to by their own kind. On page 238 (American edition) of "Orthodoxy" the following sentences are to be found: —

> There is a phrase of facile liberality uttered again and again at ethical societies and parliaments of religion: "the religions of the earth differ in rites and forms, but they are the same in what they teach." It is false: it is the opposite of the fact.

It is indeed false! After an intimate acquaintance with Ethical Societies extending over fourteen years, both in England and America, I have no hesitation in saying that Mr. Chesterton never in his life heard this moonstruck absurdity uttered in any Ethical Society; nay, he never heard it said by any sane person anywhere. It is a misrepresentation so huge and palpable that, if we did not know our Chesterton, we should be inclined to dismiss it as a deliberate falsehood. That, however, it is not. It is the expression of intellectual wilfulness; the dictum of one so accustomed to substitute ridicule for fair argument that he can no longer distinguish between them. He thinks that religious liberals *ought* to talk nonsense, in order to make them easy game for him, and accordingly (by a mental process peculiar to himself, and therefore indescribable) he arrives at the conclusion that they do.

The defects of the Chestertonian literary style have been pointed out by many critics. Our author is given to riotous exaggeration; nine times out of ten it is impossible to assume that he means what he says. His warmest friends have to apologize for him and explain him away. In the London "Spectator" of January 4, 1913, there appeared an able criticism, in which the judgment was expressed that this blemish on the work both of Mr. Chesterton and Mr. Shaw is so serious that it will debar both of them from a permanent place in literature. However this may be, it does at least constitute a serious strain upon the interest and attention of the reader. One grows weary, especially in Chesterton, of the perpetual use of mere verbalisms, of antitheses which are not antithetical, of the opposition of terms that do not exclude each other. To take the first instance that occurs to one's memory: Mr. Chesterton said, when discussing an old controversy between Ward and Huxley, that the dialectical victory really lay with Ward, but that Huxley secured the popular verdict by reason of his greater powers of literary expression. Mr. Chesterton's wholly false way of stating the case was this: "Ward could think, but Huxley could write."

This absurd opposition of perfectly compatible terms is typical of a thousand similar misjudgments. It is as though one should say, "Ward could eat, but Huxley could drink." If the writer really meant what he implies — that Ward could not write and Huxley could not think — he was guilty of an outrageous libel on both of them. So far does Mr. Chesterton carry this tone of dinner-table chaff into what purport to be serious literary and intellectual judgments, that he has no right to complain of people (as he frequently does) for refusing to take him seriously or to believe that he means what he says. In an hour's examination of his innumerable essays one could mark in the margin at least fifty things which, not being a fool, he literally *cannot* mean. He must stop his buffooneries if he dislikes their inevitable consequences. He undoubtedly deserves the crushing censure passed by Mr. Birrell on the style of Macaulay. Macaulay's style, says Mr. Birrell, was admirable for many purposes, but it had one serious defect: it was not adapted for telling the truth about anything. That is what is the matter with

Mr. Chesterton. He has many and admirable powers, but his capacity for exact accurate statement has been so long abused or disused that it now seems practically destroyed.

I have shown that he sneers at his opponents, and substitutes for serious argument an appeal to the gallery. Let me again illustrate the point by taking the first instance that comes to hand as one turns the pages of his books. I open at random the volume of papers entitled "All Things Considered," and on page 189, in an essay on "Science and Religion," I find this complete demonstration of my contention. Mr. Chesterton quotes from some unnamed exponent of the New Theology a passage to the effect that modern science had shown that there never was a historical event corresponding to the theological account of the Fall of Man. He comments upon the assertion as follows: —

It is written with earnestness and in excellent English: it must mean something. But what can it mean? *How could physical science prove that man is not depraved?* You do not cut a man open to find his sins. You do not boil him until he gives forth the unmistakable green fumes of depravity. How could physical science find any trace of *a moral fall?* What traces did the writer expect to find? Did he expect to find a fossil Eve, with a fossil apple inside her? Did he suppose that the ages would have spared for him a complete skeleton of Adam, attached to a slightly faded figleaf? [1]

[1] Italics the present writer's.

Observe the jugglery! — and remember that these are the words of one who has presumed to enter the lists in behalf of orthodoxy, and thereby professed himself familiar, at least in general outline, with the doctrines of orthodox theology. The writer he is here attacking had not suggested that physical science could find any traces of a *moral* fall. Neither had he suggested or even dreamed that science could prove that man is not depraved. He referred to evidence, not of a moral fall of man, but, explicitly, of an historical event which by orthodox theology has always been alleged to have resulted from the Fall of Man, and that an event of which, if it had occurred, physical science could not have failed to discover abundant traces. His context clearly showed that he had in mind St. Paul's theory of the Fall and its consequences. Now, according to the orthodox doctrine as expounded by St. Paul and as expressed in "Paradise Lost," the Fall of Man was an event which *"brought death into the world, and all our woe."* That is what the New Theologian was talking about. His perfectly plain meaning was, that if the orthodox doctrine were true, our science could not have failed to verify it by showing that at a certain definite epoch the phenomenon called death first took place in the world. What physical science has proved is that death has always been the correlative of life, from the far-off dawn of physical sentiency. Now, if Mr. Chesterton does not know that all orthodox Christians have, with St. Paul, understood the

Fall of Adam as the cause of mortality, then he does not know the first rudiments of what he is talking about. His treatment of his opponent in the passage I have quoted is either a piece of elephantine humour, or else it reveals an ignorance of theology which for ever disentitles him to serious attention.

It is such deliverances as these that have produced in the minds of readers that incredulity as to his seriousness which so annoys him. The only possible comment one could make is that the above-quoted farrago is barely tolerable if meant as a joke, but if meant otherwise is an unpardonable misinterpretation of his opponent.

And yet it is with theology that his most important work assumes to deal. It is true that he diplomatically abstains from claiming for "Orthodoxy" the rank of an ecclesiastical treatise. He calls it "a sort of slovenly autobiography," and one cannot ascribe the depreciatory adjective to any excess of modesty on his part. His book is by no means an ordered argument. In it, he says, he has attempted "in a vague and personal way, in a set of mental pictures rather than in a series of deductions," to state the philosophy which has enlisted his allegiance. He deliberately omits the only really vital problem — that of the seat and credentials of the authority upon which the orthodox repose their faith. And he never once grapples seriously with any one of the formidable forces arrayed against orthodoxy. The book is almost as negative in its effect as is Mr. Balfour's "Foundations of Belief." By this I mean that one might agree with almost all that Mr. Chesterton says in criticism of present-day philosophy and science, and yet find oneself destitute of the barest rag of a reason for believing in the Apostles' Creed, which, "as understood by everybody calling himself Christian until a very short time ago," he chooses as his standard of orthodoxy.

Such, indeed, is my own position. I find myself in cordial agreement with much of his attack upon certain unwarrantable assumptions and certain more or less obscure tendencies of that crude, materialistic determinism which he is pleased to call modern thought. I had passed similar strictures on them many times, long before I read Mr. Chesterton's apologetic. But he omits to notice the important fact that his own criticisms generally apply with far greater force to believers in the faith which he professes than to the modern so - called unbelievers against whom he is crusading.

In his first chapter, entitled "The Maniac," one finds a familiar fact of abnormal psychology wisely and wittily presented. I will not dwell upon the self-contradiction involved in his contending at the outset that one must not believe in oneself, and then, in the second chapter (on page 56), maintaining emphatically that one is bound to believe in oneself. Let us rather attend for a moment to the proposition that "the madman is not the man who has lost his reason. The madman is

the man who has lost everything except his reason."
The assertion, of course, is true of some madmen; and
Mr. Chesterton's conclusion that the materialist is in
danger of becoming mad in this sense is quite undeniable. But to what school of thinkers does his warning
apply half so forcibly as to the whole historic succession
of the theologians?

Having stated this truth, Mr. Chesterton buttresses
it with a misstatement. It is reasoning itself, he tells
us, — it is sheer logic, — which sends people mad.
Poetry and art, he says, are entirely compatible with
sanity; but ratiocination is the road to Hanwell. The
truth is that it is no more logic than it is art or poetry
which produces insanity. It is some impaired physiological correlative of consciousness; some defect of
brain or nerve, due to strain or overwork if not to
heredity, and quite as likely to be induced by excessive toil at art or poetry as by over-indulgence in the
logical process. And the peculiarity of the maniac is
not his reasoning, but the fact that he reasons *in vacuo*.
He has lost touch with reality. While his logic may
be irrefutable, yet it is vitiated through being based
upon untested and unverifiable premises. Doubtless
there is much akin to madness, as Mr. Chesterton
contends, in the baseless and fantastic argumenta-
tion of Haeckel and his school. Yet if one wanted to
find the crucial and glaring examples of this kind
of derangement, one would have to turn to the theologians. From Origen and Tertullian down to Jon-

athan Edwards — yes, and even John Henry Newman — one could find a depressing procession of
thinkers who, measured by Mr. Chesterton's own
standard, show every mark of that alienation from
the world of normal experience which is the diagnostic
of insanity. The Catholic theologian who asserts that,
in the economy of a merciful God, infants less than a
span long will be seen crawling on the floor of hell, is
the crowning evidence of Mr. Chesterton's contention.
He may be an admirable reasoner; but he starts from
a premise which has no relation to reality, which is
unverified and unverifiable, — because, luckily, it can
never be reduced to terms of experience.

After contending that it is reasoning which sends
men mad, Mr. Chesterton maintains that it is mysticism which keeps them sane. "As long as you have
mystery," he tells us, "you have health; when you destroy mystery you create morbidity." Most true! But
see how here the apologist's two-edged sword has
wounded him with its reverse edge. Who but the orthodox theologian has sought to destroy that mystery
which is the very life-breath of sanity? The mystic is
the man whose sense of peace in life is so real, whose
acceptance of the high privilege of being is so glad and
so spontaneous, that he willingly embraces it, with all
its unresolved discords, all its insoluble riddles. Orthodoxy is the polar antithesis of this sane mysticism.
The orthodox theologian is the man who cannot endure, who cannot even face, "the burden of unintelli-

gible things." He dares not think of the world until he has a ready-made answer to all the questions which its mystery evokes in the brooding soul. He cannot be happy without a theory, or what he calls a revelation, to explain to him the origin of things, the final goal of creation, and the destiny of his soul in a life beyond life. Let us, then, agree with Mr. Chesterton that it is mysticism which keeps men sane; but let us point out to him that in advancing this argument he has, at the very outset, clumsily annihilated the foundations of his own superstructure.

His chapter on "The Suicide of Thought" enshrines a truth as evident, and as important, as that which lies at the root of his argument about the maniac. It is perfectly true that the will-worship of Schopenhauer and Nietzsche is anti-rational, and would, if completely acted out, lead to utter futility and frustration.

But here one encounters what is perhaps the most unpardonable trick of Mr. Chesterton's method. He professes to be refuting modern thought. He alludes, it is true, to Schopenhauer and Nietzsche, but in a fashion which leaves in one's mind the gravest doubts as to the extent of his first-hand study of them; and the one representative of "modern thought" with whom he seems really familiar (apart from his friend and enemy, Mr. Shaw) is, of all persons, Mr. H. G. Wells! This, I say, is the unpardonable thing, — that Mr. Chesterton should base his indictment of what he calls modern thought on the tenth-rate futilities of a stray tale-teller trespassing in the field of philosophy, and moving about in worlds that he has never realized. Mr. H. G. Wells's book entitled "First and Last Things" is of a nature to make Englishmen blush for the intellectual reputation of their country. It displays an incapacity for philosophical thinking, a blindness to its author's own limitations, a readiness to rush in where angels fear to tread, which can only be described as shameful.

The particular absurdity upon which Mr. Chesterton fastens as an evidence of "The Suicide of Thought" is one that reveals, not suicide, but total incapacity for thought; I mean, of course, Mr. Wells's serene denial of the validity of the logical law of identity and difference, — a law presupposed in the very act of disputing it, and undeniable save in virtue of itself. If it were not true that A is either B or not B, then it would be as useless for Mr. Wells to attempt to write a novel as he has shown it to be for him to attempt to write philosophy. But to take this self-confessed vender at second-hand of the sophisms of a Cambridge schoolgirl as a representative of modern thought is not merely Chestertonian — it is also Gilbertian. It is as ludicrous as it would be to take a Pastor Russell or a ranting street-corner evangelist as a representative of Christian philosophy and theology, and ignore the master-minds of the Church —the Butlers and Newmans, the Hookers and Taylors, the Pascals and the Augustines. If Mr. Chesterton had wanted to deal justly and seriously with modern thought he should have joined battle with its real masters, from Arnold and Seeley, let us say, down to Green and Sidgwick, James and Paulsen, Bradley, Eucken and Bergson. This he has not essayed; and, pending further evidence, we may venture without undue presumption to doubt whether he can do it.

Let us remember, however, that its controversial passages are only introduced for fun, since "Orthodoxy" claims to be no more than a spiritual autobiography, and much reasoning is declared to make us mad. We are dealing with the record of a personal experience, not with a process of argument. Mr. Chesterton learned his philosophy of life from the fairy-tales, not of science, but of the nursery. In these, as he has testified many times, he found an attitude towards life which squared with his own temperament and reinforced him in his spontaneous emotional reactions upon the world in which he found himself. From them he first learned the mingled goodness and evil of the world, and the sane balance of deep discontent and yet deeper content. They taught him to doubt the tacit presuppositions of that shallow materialism which he mistakes for modern thought. They encouraged him to trust his own immediate intuition, that the really striking characteristic of the world is not its regularity, its repetition, its classifiability, but its spontaneity, its eternal eruption of individuality, its *penchant* for the unprecedented and the unclassifiable.

In short, Mr. Chesterton claims for himself that he came unconsciously to take the Christian attitude to- wards life — on the authority of fairy-tales. Before he had thought of Christian theology, he had hammered out for himself a brand-new heresy that was first cousin to it; and his subsequent development has been simply the re-discovery (as he humorously expresses it) of what had been discovered before.

Perhaps the best chapter of his fascinating story is the one entitled "The Flag of the World." It breathes a spirit of which there is a plentiful lack in our day, and affirms a truth which seems now more than ever to need reaffirming. This is the truth which saves us from the extravagances both of indiscriminate opti- mism and of pessimism. It is the fact, unquestionable as soon as it is clearly stated, that the loyalty which we owe to life is ultimate and unconditional; it is prior to and independent of any calculation of the quan- titative proportions of good and evil in the world. As the patriot does not dream of proportioning his loyalty to the precise amount of worth in his nation; as the child does not mete out his love to his parents by refer- ence to their particular degree of goodness to him, — so the cosmic patriot "accepts the universe," simply because he is in it and of it. For him, as Mr. Chesterton most wisely says, the goodness of the world is a reason for loving it, and its badness a reason for loving it still more.

But how are we to account for this mixture of good

and evil in man and nature, — in that universe which we love because we must, because of it we are a part? Mr. Chesterton finds the answer in the Christian doctrines of God, and of original sin.

How these two doctrines hang together, — how the facts of sin in man and of evil in the subhuman world are to be reconciled with the Creator's supposed attributes of omnipotence and of infinite goodness, — Mr. Chesterton very unkindly refrains from telling us; yet his silence is perhaps prudent, for the two dogmas stand opposed in eternal and irreconcilable contradiction. But of the fact of sin there is assuredly no doubt. And here Mr. Chesterton, with an inconsequence which again illustrates the incurable looseness I have complained of in his thinking, makes an illicit leap. He passes from the patent fact of sin to the alleged fact of *original* sin, which is a totally different matter. Original sin, he hardily declares, "is the only part of Christian theology which can really be proved." But how can the fact that we come into the world with impulses towards evil as well as towards good prove that we are descended from an ancestor who originally was devoid of evil impulses? No more than it can prove our descent from one who at first had no good impulses at all. Neither is this fact explained by the naïve hypothesis of a once complete goodness which became, in despite of omnipotence, inexplicably perverted into an original badness. The explanation needs more explaining than the original mystery. The facts of life no more prove the Christian doctrine than they prove metempsychosis or karma. Either of these theories will fit and explain the facts rather better than does the orthodox notion of the Fall of Man. How queerly this argument of Mr. Chesterton's illuminates for us the workings of his mind! The fault it displays is all too common among professional theologians, but one might have hoped that the adventurous literary amateur would escape it; — the fault, I mean, of talking about "proof," when he cannot produce (because he has not got) a single grain of verifiable evidence.

But life, he tells us, is itself contradictory. It is full of paradoxes, and to its paradoxes answer those of the Church. It is unreasonable, therefore, he urges, to complain of riddles in theology when these manifestly correspond to riddles of experience which are equally insoluble. His theology he takes to be "the best root of energy and sound ethics." Life demands of us an eternal revolution, the inspiration for which, he thinks, can come only from our acceptance of a doctrine of original sin which shall warn us that the best human institutions are in constant danger of being wrested into instruments of oppression. But why do we need, in our warfare against the evil tendencies within us and around us, any other stimulus than the facts themselves of experience? Or, if other stimulus be needed, how can we find it in a doctrine which is itself unverifiable, and itself, when rightly understood (as

it was, for example, by St. Augustine, the inventor of
that system of theology which Mr. Chesterton loathes
and derides under the name of Calvinism), a direct
incentive to pessimism as regards the nature of man
and his native powers for good?

Upon the vague modern doctrines of pantheism
and of the identity of man as he actually is with God,
Mr. Chesterton makes an onslaught which is brilliant
and delightful, and, I think, substantially sound. But
even here he does not reach bedrock; he cannot distinguish between the empirical self and the Self of
selves, the Man in men. The result is that he inverts
and distorts the meaning of Swinburne's "Hertha"
(a stanza of which he quotes, with his customary inaccuracy). Swinburne represents the Soul of all
things as saying to the individual man, "I am thou,
whom thou seekest to find him; find thou but thyself,
thou art I." Whereupon Mr. Chesterton comments
as follows: —

> Of which the immediate and evident deduction is
> that tyrants are as much the sons of God as Garibaldis;
> and that King Bomba of Naples, having, with the ut-
> most success, "found himself," is identical with the ulti-
> mate good in all things.

If he had taken the trouble to read thirty pages
further on in "Songs before Sunrise," he would have
discovered that Swinburne by no means identifies the
bad in man with God, or admits that all men are
divine. God is not the *totality* of the human, but its

essence, which is a very different matter; and that essence is the good. As thus: —

God, if a God there be, is the substance of men, which is
    Man.

. . . .

Not each man of all men is God, but God is the fruit of the
    whole;
Indivisible spirit and blood, indiscernible body from soul.
Not men's but Man's is the glory of Godhead, the kingdom of
    time. . . .

And later, in the same "Hymn of Man," Swinburne acknowledges (as he does in a score of passages in the same volume) that by pandering to his lower self instead of following his essential and universal self, man has sinned and failed: —

Man makes love to disaster, and woos desolation with love,
Yea, himself too hath made himself chains, and his own hands
    plucked out his eyes;
For his own soul only constrains him, his own mouth only denies.

Once again, Mr. Chesterton's criticism recoils with disastrous effect upon that theology which he supposes himself to be defending. For orthodoxy, too, has its doctrine of the identity of men with God. By its sacrament of baptism, it professes to make men "members of Christ, children of God, and inheritors of the kingdom of heaven." It assumes to *regenerate* them into that original divine nature which the first man forfeited. Between the regenerate and the unregenerate the only difference is that the one has received this sacrament, the other not. The difference is totally

unrelated to ethics and to character. Have we not
here a possible explanation of the spiritual pride and
blindness which have characterized the Church in all
ages, which underlay the practices of the Inquisitors,
and are to-day manifested, for example, in the treatment of the Jews in Holy Russia?

One has constantly to remind oneself, however, that
in "Orthodoxy" one is reading autobiography rather
than apologetic. The special interest of Mr. Chesterton's case is not logical but psychological. A revolter
by temperament, he must needs have rebelled against
the school of thought, whatever it was, in which he
happened to be reared. Because he was trained in
theological liberalism, he naturally revolted into its
opposite. From agnosticism he has leaped over to
Catholicism; and no attentive student can doubt that,
had he been reared in Catholicism, he would have
revolted just as spontaneously into agnosticism; —
as (by the grace of God) he may yet live to do: into
an agnosticism wiser and humbler than that from
which he set out. The best picture he has given us of
himself is to be found not in "Orthodoxy," but in his
freaky novel called "The Man Who Was Thursday."
The hero of that fantasy — who is, as usual, but a
mask for Mr. Chesterton himself — is described as
having "revolted into sanity," because there was
nothing else left to revolt into. And how strictly Mr.
Chesterton's own development has been an emotional
and temperamental one is perhaps shown best of all

by the lines in which he dedicates this book to his
friend Mr. Edmund Clerihew Bentley: —

A cloud was on the mind of men, and wailing went the weather,
Yea, a sick cloud upon the soul when we were boys together.
Science announced non-entity and art admired decay;
The world was old and ended; but you and I were gay.
Round us in antic order their [1] crippled vices came —
Lust that had lost its laughter, fear that had lost its shame.
Like the white lock of Whistler, that lit our aimless gloom,
Men showed their own white feather as proudly as a plume.
Life was a fly that faded, and death a drone that stung;
The world was very old indeed when you and I were young.
They twisted even decent sin to shapes not to be named:
Men were ashamed of honour; but we were not ashamed.
Weak if we were and foolish, not thus we failed, not thus;
When that black Baal blocked the heavens, he had no hymns
   from us.
Children we were — our forts of sand were even weak as we;
High as they went we piled them up to break that bitter sea.
Fools as we were in motley, all jangling and absurd,
When all church bells were silent our cap and bells were heard.

 · · · · · · · · ·

But we were young; we lived to see God break their [1] bitter
   charms,
God and the good Republic come riding back in arms: [1]
We have seen the City of Mansoul, even as it rocked, relieved —
Blessed are they who did not see, but, being blind, believed.

 · · · · · · · · ·

Between us, by the peace of God, such truth can now be
   told;
Yea, there is strength in striking root, and good in growing
   old.
We have found common things at last, and marriage and a
   creed,
And I may safely write it now, and you may safely read.

     [1] *Sic.*

Temperament, then, and that sanity of ethical intuition in which we have found his most admirable attribute, are the factors that explain his change of attitude. And surely he was right to revolt against what he, although mistakenly, imagined to be the inevitable tendencies of modern thought. The doctrine of the world-machine, the doctrine of mechanical determinism, the doctrine of the absolute dependence of mind on body, the new mythology in which the hypostatized abstractions called Heredity and Environment replace the Adam and Satan of the old mythology, — all these unverified and unverifiable dogmas lay on the mind of men, and formed a sick cloud upon the soul, when he and his friend were boys together. But was it not enough to expel these harpies, without replacing them by a brood of darkness equally phantasmagorical, equally crushing and annihilating in their impact upon the spirit of man? For this is what Mr. Chesterton has done. His orthodoxy is new to him; he finds it "all a wonder and a wild desire." But he will find sooner or later, if he scrutinizes it as ruthlessly as he did the ideas current around him in his boyhood, that he has escaped Charybdis only to be hopelessly shipwrecked upon Scylla.

There is one part of Mr. Chesterton's argument which shows almost grotesquely how dangerous it is to try to defend orthodoxy when you do not yet quite know what orthodoxy is. The gist of his spiritual autobiography is that he invented Christianity for himself; whereafter he discovered with blank amazement that the system which he had painfully hewn out had antedated his own existence by some eighteen hundred years. "I did try," he says, "to found a heresy of my own; and when I had put the last touches to it, I discovered that it was orthodoxy." Behold how ingenuously the inexpert player kicks over his wicket in his anxiety to score! The whole contention of orthodox theology is that its scheme is so wonderful, so supernatural, that the unaided powers of the natural man could never have shaped it. It is based upon revelation from on high, and is declared to be of such a nature as to carry within itself the evidence of its extra-mundane origin. That modern science which Mr. Chesterton so ungratefully derides has demonstrated, as against this claim, that the orthodox scheme is but one of a series of blundering hypotheses invented to account for the obvious facts of life; and he concedes that men *could* have invented it — because he did so himself! He does not lay claim to a special private revelation, vouchsafed to him alone, like St. Paul's or Lord Herbert of Cherbury's. He, Gilbert Chesterton, tried to found a heresy of his own; and when he had put the finishing touches to it, he discovered that it was orthodoxy!

His amazement, therefore, at finding that Christian dogma fitted his feelings and answered his questions, is entirely gratuitous. The reason why it does so is simply because other men in other times, of like nature with himself, did exactly what he claims to have done. They too founded a heresy of their own, and when they had put the last touches to it, they made it orthodoxy by calling it so and murdering all gainsayers. There is nothing more mysterious in the process than there would be if a coat, made to fit a man of Mr. Chesterton's height and girth (let us say, Velazquez's Cavalier), having accidentally survived the centuries, should now be found to fit Mr. Chesterton. The makers of orthodoxy cut their theology to fit their souls; why then should it not fit Mr. Chesterton's, since his happens to be of the same size?

His objection to the modern doctrines of materialism, mechanical determinism, and the like, is that they are, or may easily become, the allies of oppression. I fully admit the possibility. But how has Mr. Chesterton succeeded in overlooking the obtrusive fact that his beloved orthodoxy has, throughout history, been fifty times more the ally of oppression than they? Was it materialism that decimated the Jews of Spain and Portugal, and then broke faith with them and expelled them? Was it modern scientific thought that obliterated the native races of Spanish America, and made a moral and a physical desert, in that mad rush for God and gold which was Spanish imperialism? Did mechanical determinism give rise to the massacre of St. Bartholomew, or revoke the Edict of Nantes? Were the fires of Smithfield, the witch-burnings and heresy-huntings which blacken the history of

England and Scotland, produced by the doctrines of Haeckel or the puzzle-headed scepticisms of Mr. H. G. Wells? I will not join in the cheap and easy amusement of flinging mud at a great historic institution like the Catholic Church; but I cannot lightly set aside the temperate and irrefragable indictment which Lecky brings against her, that she has "shed more innocent blood, and caused more unmerited suffering, than any other institution known to history."

Mr. Chesterton has an inborn love of liberty, a hatred of oppression, which entitle him to our profound and grateful respect. No man has battled more bravely than he against the hypocritical tyrannies of our present-day political and economic systems. In any purely moral issue, in any battle for genuine freedom, he is almost certain to be found on the right side; and when he goes wrong — when, for instance, we find him joining in the mediæval barbarism, recently revived in England, of Jew-baiting — we can generally make a pretty shrewd guess at the identity of those of his fellow-Catholics who have misled him. This characteristic in him entitles us to ask why he has embraced a doctrine which has, throughout the history of fifteen hundred years, been enthroned in power and allied with every kind of oppression; a doctrine whose custodians have slaughtered both souls and bodies in the interests of their spiritual despotism and their Church's temporal power. How is it that he is so ready to tell us of the witch-burnings practised in Puritan

Massachusetts, and so oblivious of the fact that where Puritanism has slain its thousands, Catholicism has burnt and tortured its tens of thousands?

In a recent issue of the "Dublin Review," Mr. Wilfrid Ward testified to the originality of the apologetic work done by Mr. Chesterton in "Orthodoxy." This was uncommonly generous of Mr. Ward, who has himself done such very fresh and interesting work of the same order, in his "Witnesses to the Unseen" and elsewhere. No one will dispute his claim so far as it relates to the manner of the book; but as regards its matter, it is our duty to remind a busy and forgetful generation that Mr. Chesterton has not the slightest claim to originality. His whole book (in so far as it forgets to be an autobiography and becomes a polemic) is nothing but a rehash of two arguments which will be found more ably presented, backed up by far deeper philosophic insight and far greater power of rational thought, in two of the classics of Christian apologetics: the "Analogy" of Bishop Butler and the "Apologia" of Cardinal Newman.

Bishop Butler's masterly work is little else than a sustained and powerful insistence that the dogmas of Christianity fit and explain the facts of life better than did the complacent optimism of the Deists, against whom he contended. And the great Cardinal's memorable book anticipates and presses home (with destructive effect as against Protestantism) the danger of that very suicide of thought which alarms Mr. Chesterton.

With incomparable lucidity, Newman shows that an infallible Bible is useless and dangerous unless backed up and interpreted by an infallible visible authority. Scripture, he tells us, is impotent to "make a stand against the wild, living intellect of man." The infallibility of the Church was supernaturally designed "to restrain that freedom of thought, which of course in itself is one of the greatest of our natural gifts, and *to rescue it from its own suicidal excesses.*" This is, indeed, like Butler's, only an *argumentum ad hominem;* but neither Butler nor Newman has ever been or ever will be answered effectively from the point of view of those against whom each wrote. Readers, therefore, who wish to see the argument for orthodoxy at its best, as it is presented by the great masters of Christian thought, will turn to Newman and Butler, to Pascal, Chillingworth and Hooker. After reading these, they will see in Mr. Chesterton's amateur apologetics nothing but a psychological curiosity, to be read, like his novels, for amusement, in some slight degree perhaps for edification, but not at all for instruction.

For, after all, we are left with the gravest reasons for suspecting not only Mr. Chesterton's argumentative powers, but actually the soundness of his orthodoxy. It is alarming to find that in his opinion Christian theology is "sufficiently summarized in the Apostles' Creed." One's apprehensions are awakened by the assertion that "when the word 'orthodoxy' is used here it means the Apostles' Creed, as understood by *everybody calling himself Christian* until a very short time ago." To what good Catholic can this possibly be satisfactory? If we were addicted to Mr. Chesterton's habit of flippant paradox, we should declare that the Apostles' Creed is not orthodox. That would certainly be quite in his manner. Caring, however, more for truth than for startlingness of statement, let us content ourselves with the moderate and incontrovertible assertion that the Apostles' Creed does not sufficiently summarize Christian theology; and no Catholic theologian who knew his business would admit for a moment that belief in it was sufficient to make a man a Christian. No doubt it contains a great deal more doctrine than was believed in by St. Paul and the writers of the Synoptic Gospels, but that only shows what a wonderful thing "development" may be in an unchanging Church. The successors of St. Peter have made the faith once delivered to him and his colleagues into something richer and stranger than he ever dreamed of; and if St. Peter could reappear to-day, with only such beliefs as he held when he died, not a Catholic bishop in Christendom would confirm him — much less admit him to Orders.

For all that, however, the so-called Apostles' Creed is an entirely unsatisfactory statement of the Church's position; and the Church has tacitly admitted the fact. For if the Apostolic formula expressed its theology adequately, why was it found necessary in subsequent Councils to proceed to the formulation first of the Nicene, and afterwards of the Athanasian Creed, — to say nothing of the Tridentine Decrees, and even later definitions of matters of faith? The truth is that the Apostles' Creed omits the very vitals of orthodoxy. It does not even assert that God the Father is a person, or that the Holy Ghost is God. It contains no allusion to original sin; it fails to affirm the deity of Jesus; it makes no mention of the Trinity. It has no glimmer of a reference to the sacraments, to the authority of the Church or of Scripture, or to any doctrine distinctive of the Catholic Church as compared with the Protestant sects. So that even if Mr. Chesterton succeeded in proving (what he has deliberately abstained from trying to prove) that there is valid historic and philosophic ground for believing in the Apostles' Creed, we should still be as devoid as ever of adequate warrant for following him into the Church's fold.

The lamest of Mr. Chesterton's many lame arguments is his maladroit defence of miracle. In this part of his book he substitutes sneering for argument even more liberally than elsewhere; and his case for miracles, if it may be called a case for them at all, works down to the simple - minded contentions, first that miracles happen to-day as much as in the past, and secondly that you must accept unreservedly the assertion of any peasant who informs you that he has seen a ghost. You are to believe not only in his veracity, —

which may well be above suspicion, — but also in his competence to interpret his experience! The whole discussion is rendered profitless by the fact that Mr. Chesterton never condescends to inform us what he means by a miracle. Now the word miracle, as used historically in Christian theology to describe the wonderful deeds of Jesus and his apostles, means a breach of the phenomenal sequences of nature. It is illegitimately used when applied to any event, however rare or even totally unprecedented, which arose naturally from adequate phenomenal antecedents. Anything which would happen again if the circumstances conditioning it were repeated, is not a miracle; not even though it were a case of resurrection from the dead, or of human generation without the normal process of sexual fecundation. A perfectly trivial circumstance, on the other hand, such as the bending of a blade of grass, or the freezing of a drop of water, would be a miracle if it occurred independently of its accustomed context of physical antecedents and concomitants.

Mr. Chesterton is inexcusably mistaken in thinking that those who reject the Christian miracles do so by reason of an *a priori* conviction that miracles either cannot or do not happen.[1] They reject them for lack

[1] In the debate held at the Little Theatre in London on January 21st, 1914, as a part of the "boom," referred to on p. 43, which was got up to save *Magic* from failing, Mr. Hilaire Belloc committed himself to the astonishing statement that Huxley rejected miracles not for lack of evidence, but because he denied the existence of any "personality behind nature," and therefore held them to be antecedently incredible. A little later he affirmed that to-day "almost all the rich

of evidence, just as they reject any alleged natural
event, — such as the discovery of America by ancient
Jews, affirmed by Mormonism, or the founding of
Rome by Romulus and Remus, — for which there is
no adequate documentary or other historical warrant.
Mr. Chesterton, on the other hand, like his fellow-
Catholics, does not base his acceptance of the miracles
of Galilee and Lourdes upon the amount and kind of
evidence which can be adduced in their support. He
believes in them in virtue of an *a priori* doctrine.[1] If
it were not so, — if it were merely a question of evidence, — he would have to accept a host of alleged

are on the side of atheism." Both assertions contain exactly the same
amount of truth — and that is none at all. Huxley never in his life
denied either the existence of a "personality behind nature" or the
antecedent possibility of miracle. He did deny that the particular
miracles related in the New Testament, and others vouched for by
Catholic tradition, have any such evidence as to justify belief in them.
But that is a totally distinct question. The immoral levity with which
a cultured man like Mr. Belloc misrepresents views he does not hold
is a precious commentary on the ethical influence of his Church. We
know he is a cultured man, because we have his own word for it. The
essays on *Agnosticism* and on *The Value of Witness to the Miraculous*
in which Huxley made his position transparently clear can be obtained at any public library, and can be purchased in England
(where books are cheap) in an excellently printed edition published by
Messrs. Macmillan for sixpence. So there is absolutely no excuse for
Mr. Belloc.

[1] His brother Cecil fully admitted this in the debate referred to in
the preceding footnote. Dealing with the miracle of the Virgin Birth,
he conceded that there is not — as indeed there could not be — any
human evidence for it whatever. But, as he quite correctly added,
Catholics believe it because they hold it more probable that it happened than that the Church should be mistaken or should wish to
deceive. Which amounts to saying that they believe whatever the
Church chooses to tell them. The *circulus in probandi* is complete.
The Church is credible because it is attested by miracle — and miracle
is credible because it is attested by the Church.

pagan miracles which he now rejects, but which in truth (Church authority apart) are far better attested than most of those which he accepts.

It is, of course, only a vulgar confusion of thought, as Matthew Arnold long since pointed out, which sees in miracles any evidence to anything beyond themselves. If a man walked upon the sea, that would prove nothing except the fact that he could walk upon the sea; it would add no jot or tittle of weight to any statements he might make about the nature of God or the life of the soul after death. The procedure of those Christians who have accepted the teachings of Jesus Christ because they believed that he had been able to still the winds and transmute water into wine is an instance of inconsequential reasoning due to philosophic illiteracy.

Those who reject the New Testament miracles need not take either the critical attitude of Hume (who held that in any given case it was more probable that the testimony was false or mistaken than that the alleged miracle occurred) or the standpoint of Kant, who maintained that unless an event were strictly articulated in the causal series, it could not enter into human perception, — causality being a necessary form of all thought and experience, or, as Professor Adler calls it, a "functional finality." We can dispose of the whole question of the New Testament miracles on the ground of their lack of historic support. It is not too much to say, at this time of day, that a man who professes to believe in them, in the full, literal, unhesitating way in which mediæval Christians believed in them, is a man who either cannot or will not penetrate to the bottom of the discussion. Mr. Chesterton is such a man. He has not *approfondi les choses*. He does instead what he unjustly accuses Matthew Arnold of doing: he "recites his dogma with implicit faith."

To sum up: Our objection to orthodoxy is, first, that it is unverifiable, either by history or by present-day experience; and secondly, that history proves it to have been actually disastrous in its consequences for humanity, in the very way in which Mr. Chesterton thinks modern thought may be disastrous. It is, as we have said, an unsupported guess at an insoluble mystery.

Mr. Chesterton ought to have called his book not "Orthodoxy," but "How I Found God." For it is in truth the story of his attainment of peace, of his tardy and hard-won reconciliation with the eternal order of things. Here, on the ground of experience, the religious liberals at whom he gibes can join hands with him; for they too, in this sense, have found God. And they have found a deeper truth than Mr. Chesterton's; — the truth that for real reconciliation with life no ecclesiastical dogma is necessary, and no answer to the insatiable questionings of man's metaphysical craving. The truly redeemed man is not he who has attained a theory which solves for him the mysteries of being, but he who has reached the point where he no longer yearns for a solution of the riddles. In the intimate realities of experience itself, — in the loyalty of comrades, in the love of husband and wife, in the mystery of birth and the joy of parenthood; above all, in the sublimity of the moral law, at once consoling and energizing, we find the divine: we attain both the peace that passes understanding and the inspiration for the unending battle with evil. We rejoice with Mr. Chesterton in the joy that he has found, though we regret his manifest inability to distinguish between his experience and the muddled and cramping framework of theory into which he has forced it. The God that he has found, the God in whom he truly lives and has his being, is not the God of the Athanasian Creed; it is the much more real and potent factor which inspires the lofty lines of Mr. Zangwill: —

> God lives as much as in the days of yore,
> In fires of human love and work and song,
> In wells of human tears that pitying throng,
> In thunder-clouds of human wrath at wrong.
>
> Perchance, O ye that toil on, though forlorn,
> By your souls' travail, your own noble scorn,
> The very God ye crave is being born.

CHAPTER III

IT wás wisely remarked some years ago by the late Professor Friedrich Paulsen that "an age is characterized more by the books which it reads than by those which it writes." Paulsen offered this dictum as his justification for devoting a good deal of space to exposing the network of fallacies and self-contradictions which make up the great bulk of Ludwig Büchner's once universally known, but now almost forgotten, treatise entitled "Force and Matter." This consideration also led him, in the year 1900, to devote a lengthy article in the "Preussische Jahrbücher" to a minute analysis of the positions set forth in Ernst Haeckel's treatise entitled "The Riddles of the Universe," published in 1899. After completely shattering the pretensions of Haeckel to rank as a philosopher, and exposing the egregious incompetence and the blatant dogmatism to which almost every page of his volume bears witness, Dr. Paulsen ended his essay with the following notable words: —

> If every nation and every age has not only the government but also the literature that it deserves to have, yet, nevertheless, the responsibility for these things lies upon all who have part in them. I have read this book with

burning shame — with shame for the level of general culture and of philosophic culture among our people. That such a book was possible — that it could have been written, printed, bought, read, admired, and believed by the nation that possesses a Kant, a Goethe, a Schopenhauer: this is painful.[1]

Already in 1900, when this essay of Paulsen's appeared, the book of which it treated had obtained a wide notoriety. Since then, however, it has enjoyed a distribution probably unequalled in the history of the world by any other treatise dealing with such serious themes as those which it handles. It has been translated into no less than twenty-four languages, including Sanscrit. The publisher of the English translation recently informed me that he had sold over a quarter of a million copies of it in England and the British Colonies, the great majority of which had been disposed of in England. Cheap editions of it, excellently printed, can be obtained in every European country, and would be available also in America, but for the unintelligent tax on knowledge, by means of which cheap literature, good as well as bad, is excluded

[1] "Hat jedes Volk und jede Zeit, wie die Regierung, so auch die Literatur, die sie zu haben verdienen, nun so ist damit auch Jedem, der an ihr Theil hat, die Mitverantwortlichkeit dafür auferlegt. Ich habe mit brennender Scham dieses Buch gelesen, mit Scham über den Stand der allgemeinen Bildung und der philosophischen Bildung unseres Volks. Dass ein solches Buch möglich war, dass es geschrieben, gedruckt, gekauft, gelesen, bewundert, geglaubt werden konnte bei dem Volk, das einen Kant, einen Goethe, einen Schopenhauer besitzt, dass ist schmerzlich." — "Ernst Haeckel als Philosoph," in *Preussische Jahrbücher*, 1900.

from this country. And not only has the book been widely bought, but it has been seized upon as a sort of new gospel by immense circles of the working class, who seem, for some unfathomable reason, to regard it as a message of good tidings and great joy to them. Multitudes of artisans in England (I limit my assertion to England because only there can I speak from first-hand personal knowledge) have studied this book with the same kind of fervour and devotion as their forbears gave to the study of the Bible. They have naturally also studied it just as unintelligently. It is known to many who have hardly ever read another serious book in their lives, and who consequently are entirely unable to read it critically or form any adequate estimate of its scientific and philosophic value. The result is that although the book is scientifically old-fashioned and philosophically beneath contempt, it is yet regarded by these multitudinous readers as the very latest and maturest wisdom of the human spirit — as being, indeed, what its author modestly calls it, the "ripe fruit of the tree of knowledge."

The qualities which explain this enormous popularity are not difficult to detect. In the first place, the book is written with great pugnacity, and therefore cannot fail to appeal to the combative instinct which is strong in us all, and especially in the mentally undisciplined. It abounds in sweeping denunciations, not only of priests and priestcraft, but of leaders in any branch of knowledge who dare to suggest that there are or can be in the universe any questions that have not been completely answered by the doctrine of Darwin — more particularly as developed and transmogrified by the prophet of Jena. What is more, although it purports to deal with all the mysteries of time and eternity, of matter and spirit, and either to solve or to point the way to the solution of the seven riddles of the universe which still remained outstanding in 1899, it nevertheless does not contain a single sentence which would be beyond the immediate comprehension of any intelligent artisan, as soon as he had mastered the glossary which is thoughtfully provided in the English translation. This means that the book unconsciously flatters the vanity of the illiterate. It makes them think that their previous inability to grasp the problems of philosophy was due not to any shortcomings of their own, but to the lack of lucidity in the writing of the philosophers. It also gives them an entirely baseless feeling of having learned a great deal and gained new insight.

In no other way can one explain the almost rapturous eulogies poured out upon Haeckel by so variously gifted a man as Mr. Robert Blatchford, the editor of a bright and deservedly popular English Socialist weekly paper called the "Clarion." It was to the "Clarion's" trumpeting that the success of the English translation of "Die Welträtsel" was mainly due. About the time when Mr. Blatchford's first article upon it appeared, I read an interview with him, in which he made the very significant admission that he could not understand a single word that he read in Kant. I quote him from memory, and therefore with something less than verbal exactness, but I am quite certain that the purport of his remark was as follows: "I once wasted six shillings on Kant's 'Critique of the Pure Reason,' and after an hour or two I threw it into the fire. What is the use of wasting time over such a ridiculous and unintelligible metaphysical dream?"

This little piece of frank autobiography, coming from Mr. Blatchford, gives us the clue to the backwardness of the masses as regards philosophy, and their readiness to fall down and worship the first glib and confident pseudo-philosophic charlatan who chances to present himself. Kant is hard to read, not only because of his seriously defective literary style, but also because he had a first-hand vision of the unplumbed mysteries which surround the soul of man on every side. Haeckel, on the other hand, is easy to read, because he wields the pen of a ready writer; he never pauses to make subtle distinctions (but only because he never sees them); and he has never had any glimpse of the vision of mystery which haunted the mind of Kant, as it has haunted the deepest minds of humanity, from before the days of Socrates and Plato down to the days of Rudolf Eucken and Henri Bergson. To quote again from Paulsen's essay, Haeckel, "since Darwinism solved for him the prob-

lem of the origin of species, sees no more problems, but
only ready-made solutions." [1]

The success of Haeckel, then, is exactly like that
of the cheap-jack Dr. Schutzmacher, in Mr. Bernard
Shaw's play of "The Doctor's Dilemma." Schutzmacher, it will be remembered, having begun with
no capital, had piled up a fortune before he had
reached middle life. Asked how he had worked this
miracle, he replied that it had been done by painting
upon his shop window the words, "Advice and medicine, sixpence. Cure guaranteed." Obviously, as he
says, when people go to the doctor what they want is
a cure, and so of course they will go in greatest numbers to the man who is ready to guarantee them what
they want. Thus it is, even with intelligent working-
men, such as those who form the rank and file of the
great German Social Democratic party, the English
Independent Labour Party, the trade unions, and the
like. These men (in common with most men of other
classes) have but slight equipment for forming an intelligent judgment on the merits of a book which professes to explain to them the riddles of the world, just
as they have for deciding between the various doctors
who seek their patronage. Their one criterion, naturally, apart from cheapness, is the confidence with
which their patronage is claimed.

[1] "Er sieht, seitdem ihm der Darwinismus das Problem der Ent-
stehung der Arten aufgelöst hat, nirgends mehr Probleme, sondern nur
bereite Lösungen."

Their readiness to fall into the snare of pseudo-philosophers like Haeckel is the not unjust Nemesis of the neglect of the human intellect by the Christian Church through eighteen hundred years. Had the Church not been so stupidly convinced that there was only one saviour of the world — had it seen that humanity needed the method and secret of Socrates as much as it needed the method and secret of Jesus — this all-pervading illiteracy would have been eliminated centuries ago. As it is, the masses are indebted, and know themselves to be indebted, to the modern secular spirit even for the rudimentary education which is nowadays given to them. The orthodox Church has been not only indifferent but actively and criminally hostile to popular education. In Europe to this day orthodoxy and illiteracy go hand in hand together. Popular ignorance and popular devotion to the Church are at their maximum in countries like Russia, Portugal, Spain and Southern Italy. In England, the establishment of free schools by the Government was achieved in the teeth of every kind of hostility, continued through decades, on the part of the authorities of the Established Church, which, having set up, for the purpose of inculcating its doctrines, a system of "national" schools, utterly inadequate in accommodation and inefficient in secular teaching, sought to prevent the allocation of public funds for the establishment or support of any other schools. And at this moment the British public schools are still held back, cramped and thwarted, and the national educational system remains disastrously incomplete and inefficient, because of the insensate squabble between the Tweedledum of Anglicanism and the Tweedledee of the non-established sects, over the exact form of dogmatic instruction to be given at the public expense. Preachers of every denomination to-day deplore the violent antagonism of the working classes to orthodox religion, and, too late, they are lamenting the sway of writers like Haeckel over the minds of these classes. The responsibility, however, lies at the door of the Church, which has always been the educator of the nations of Europe, and therefore cannot disclaim culpability for the miserable results of its agelong monopoly.

What the preacher chiefly deplores in the influence of Professor Haeckel is the childish materialism which this author shares with and intensifies in his readers. But this is only an illustration of the Church's long neglect of its duty. In so far as Haeckel and his disciples are materialists, they are in no wise different from the mass of their Christian opponents. For popular Christianity (as distinguished from philosophic and ethical Christianity) has never been anything but what Matthew Arnold bluntly but accurately called it: a materialistic fairy-tale. It has perverted and petrified the metaphors of its Founder into hard, literal statements of fact. Its central sacrament, the Eucharist, is an inexcusable literalization of his poetical figures of speech. It has never taught men, because it has never understood, how to escape from the materialistic point of view. Its hell and heaven of physical torment and delight, its fantastic doctrine of the resurrection of the body (repeated every day, in this twentieth century, by thousands of priests and millions of laymen who know it to be baseless and absurd), its Sultan-like God seated on an actual throne, enjoying throughout eternity the flatteries of his prostrate worshippers — what is all this but a stark materialism, on the mental level of savages and children?

I do not for a moment deny that there has been, all through the Christian ages, a tiny minority of believers who appraised this fairy - tale at its true worth; but the Church has never told the truth to the people, and it refuses to-day to tell them the truth, although the results of its persistence in hyp- notizing and deceiving them are visible on every hand. Only to-day have candidates for Anglican ordination been released from declaring their unfeigned belief in every word contained in the canonical scriptures — a declaration which nobody outside a lunatic asy- lum could make sincerely. Within the last few years, two English Bishops have combined to inhibit the Reverend J. M. Thompson, of Magdalen College, Oxford, from preaching, because he had dared to set forth, in his excellent volume on "Miracles in the New Testament," the truths, undeniable by competent scholars, that the New Testament miracles are devoid of evidence, that Jesus Christ never claimed to perform miracles, and that miracles are, in any case, entirely worthless as evidence to anything beyond themselves.

The Churches, then, having for ages imposed on the nations one huge materialistic myth, have no right to be surprised at the deplorable fact that the moment the masses break loose from their leading-strings, they embrace another materialistic myth. Having been lashed into unquestioning docility to one Pope and one sacred book, they escape only to follow a fresh self-constituted pope and to believe in the literal inspiration of *his* sacred book. Why should they not? For the task of self-direction they have never had any training from their ecclesiastical masters. They are like the three million so-called free voters of Mexico, ostensibly entrusted with the privileges and responsibilities of republican citizenship. That illiterate nation, incapable of self-government, is doomed either to be controlled from abroad or to be for many a day the shuttlecock of a series of usurpers of the type either of Porfirio Diaz or of Madero and Huerta. Exactly so is it in the proletarian republic of letters and of religion. Professor Haeckel, with his world-wide influence and his transparent incompetence, is the precise analogue of a Mexican dictator.

I am aware that Haeckel's English translator, in a preface to the fifth English edition, declares that the prophet of Jena is not a materialist. "For him," says Mr. McCabe, "mind is *not* a product of matter, but something developing concurrently with matter." The good faith of the assertion need not be questioned, because Dr. Haeckel's philosophic oracles are a perpetual seesaw of self-contradiction. He certainly does say in one place, "We hold, with Goethe, that 'matter cannot exist and be operative without spirit, nor spirit without matter.'" Such an assertion, isolated from its context, looks impressive; but it becomes less so when we find in the very next sentence that the "spirit" he talks about is identical with the physical energy of the inorganic world. It is a mode of the very same force which is otherwise manifested as gravitation, electricity and the like. And how can his translator have succeeded in forgetting the innumerable sentences of unqualified dogmatic materialism which he himself had first read in the German and then faithfully reproduced in English? For one sentence which seems to be susceptible of an idealistic or dualistic interpretation, there are a hundred in every chapter which absolutely exclude anything but materialistic monism. In turning Haeckel's pages one drops across dozens of sentences like the following. He is describing the brain as the organ of consciousness, and, having depicted the "sense centres," he goes on to talk about "the four great thought centres, or centres of association, *the real organs of mental life;* they are those highest instruments of

psychic activity that PRODUCE THOUGHT AND CON-
SCIOUSNESS." [1] These are the words of the writer
whose translator, in a preface to the book containing
them, declares that he does not regard mind as a
product of matter! Yet thought and consciousness
are *produced* by the thought centres of the brain!
Comment would perhaps not be superfluous, if only
it were not impossible.

This philosopher who is not a materialist, and does
not regard mind as a product of body, writes elsewhere
(in his chapter on "The Evolution of the World")
the following profound summary of his new gospel of
hope and inspiration for the masses: —

It seems to me that these modern discoveries as to the
periodic decay and re-birth of cosmic bodies, which we
owe to the most recent advance of physics and astronomy,
associated with the law of substance, are especially important in giving us a clear insight into the universal
cosmic process of evolution. In their light our earth
shrinks into the slender proportions of a "mote in the
sunbeam," of which unnumbered millions chase each
other through the vast depths of space. Our own "human nature," which exalted itself into an image of God
in its anthropistic illusion, sinks to the level of that of a
placental mammal, which has no more value for the universe at large than the ant, the fly of a summer's day,
the microscopic infusorium, or the smallest bacillus.
Humanity is but a transitory phase of the evolution of
the eternal substance, *a particular phenomenal form of
matter and energy*, the true proportion of which we soon

[1] *Die Welträtsel*, chap. x, p. 65 of 5th English edition.

perceive when we set it on the background of infinite space and eternal time.[1]

It will perhaps not be superfluous if we take a glance at the marvellous process of reasoning which leads up to this triumphant demonstration of the nothingness of man, who is thus declared to be only a form of matter and physical energy. It is well to remind the reader that Haeckel — although, like Sir Ray Lankester, Mr. Hugh Elliot, and indeed all his followers, he is perpetually sneering at the philosophers — professes in this work to be speaking as a philosopher. This school thinks and says repeatedly that all the metaphysicians, from Plato downwards, have contrib-

[1] My quotation is taken, with only two small corrections, from Mr. Joseph McCabe's English translation. The italics are mine. In order, however, that the reader may see how even more pessimistic and materialistic Haeckel is than his excessively loyal English advocate makes him seem, I append the paragraph in the original: —

"Besonders wichtig für die klare Einsicht in den universalen kosmischen Entwickelungsprozess sind diese modernen Vorstellungen über periodisch wechselnden Untergang und Neubildung der Weltkörper. Unsere Mutter Erde schrumpft dabei auf den Wert eines winzigen 'Sonnenstäubchens' zusammen, wie deren ungezählte Millionen im unendlichen Weltenraum umherjagen. Unser eigenes 'Menschenwesen,' welches in seinem anthropistischen Grössenwahn sich als 'Ebenbild Gottes' verherrlicht, sinkt zur Bedeutung eines plazentalen Säugetieres hinab, welches nicht mehr Wert für das ganze Universum besitzt als die Ameise und die Eintagsfliege, als das mikroskopische Infusorium und der winzigste Bazillus. Auch wir Menschen sind nur vorübergehende Entwickelungszustände der ewigen Substanz, individuelle Erscheinungsformen der Materie und Energie, deren *Nichtigkeit* wir begreifen, wenn wir sie dem unendlichen Raum und der ewigen Zeit gegenüberstellen."

That word "Nichtigkeit" was more than even Mr. McCabe could stand. He has softened Haeckel's assertion of the *nothingness* of humanity into the phrase, "the *true proportion* of which we soon perceive," etc.

uted nothing of the slightest value to human thought or human life. It thinks that metaphysics, together with orthodox theology, should be relegated to the cosmic lumber-room, along with all the other outgrown superstitions of the childhood of the race. Yet, despite the preposterous inconsistency of this attitude with Haeckel's own pretensions to found a philosophic system, it is about this latter pretension that he is concerned. In the original, his work bears the sub-title, "Gemeinverständliche Studien über monistische Philosophie." The English version changes the main title and omits the sub-title altogether.

My purpose renders it necessary to insist upon this aspect of Haeckel's book. This teacher, who in philosophy is everything by turns and nothing long; who, without knowing it, is successively idealist, materialist, dualist and monist; who undertakes, with the cocksure confidence of a city schoolboy, to derive the subject from the object, and thereby to annihilate the spiritual self-determination of mankind, is, in spite of his scorn for metaphysics, himself a metaphysician. He has his own theory of the relation of thought to being, and of the genesis, nature and limitations of human knowledge. If he spoke merely as a specialist in biology, and confined himself to statements verifiable by the methods of that science, it would be beyond my competence to deal with him. He is eminent in his own special field, and he made, many years ago, important and valuable additions to our biological knowledge. But he is not satisfied with the reputation which entitles him to speak as one having authority about sea-squirts and radiolaria. He must needs lay down the law to us, not only about all the physical sciences, but also about comparative religion, Biblical criticism, Christian origins, epistemology, and a dozen other subjects of which he knows practically nothing, and the fundamental principles of which he shows himself incapable of understanding.

Lest this criticism seem too sweeping, let me illustrate it by a single instance. The earlier editions of the "Riddles of the Universe," in English as well as German, contained a chapter on "Science and Christianity," in which Professor Haeckel undertook to inform his popular audience about Christian origins, the formation of the Gospel canon, and a number of kindred matters. His presentation of these was so tasteless, illiterate and untrue that the whole section had afterwards to be rewritten for him by his English translator. Prior to this kindly doctoring — that is, at the time when Haeckel's book was written by himself and not by somebody else — it contained the following learned description of the formation of the canon of the Gospels: —

As to the four canonical Gospels, we now know that they were selected from a host of contradictory and forged manuscripts of the first three centuries by the three hundred and eighteen Bishops who assembled at the Council of Nicæa in 327. The entire list of Gospels numbered forty; the canonical list contains four. As the contending and mutually abusive Bishops could not agree about the choice, they determined to leave the selection to a miracle. They put all the books (according to the "Synodicon" of Pappus) together underneath the altar, and prayed that the apocryphal books of human origin might remain there, and the genuine inspired books might be miraculously placed on the table of the Lord. And that, says tradition, really occurred! The three synoptic Gospels (Matthew, Mark and Luke — all written *after* them, not *by* them, at the beginning of the second century) and the very different fourth Gospel (ostensibly "after" John, written about the middle of the second century) leaped on the table, and were thenceforth recognized as the inspired (with their thousand mutual contradictions) foundations of Christian doctrine.[1]

It is scarcely necessary to say that this farrago of ignorant nonsense was not allowed to pass unchallenged in Germany. Professor Friedrich Loofs of Halle promptly denounced Haeckel, and in doing so deliberately chose such language as would make it possible for Haeckel, if he so desired, to prosecute his critic for libel. This Haeckel never thought fit to do; but the controversy disclosed the interesting fact that the whole of his information about early Christianity and the development of the Church had been derived from a tenth-rate "free-thought" book by an obscure English journalist, of which the German translation

[1] *Op. cit.*, chap. XVII, pp. 319–20, English translation, 2d edition, 1901.

was even worse than the original. No such crushing exposure of presumptuous ignorance was ever made before in the case of a man of academic training and career, who had won for himself deserved honours in his own field.

I met in Jena in 1909 some university students who, having formerly been enthusiastic disciples of Haeckel, had abandoned their allegiance in disgust because they were convinced that he had deliberately "faked" some of the pictures which illustrated his chapters on human phylogeny and embryology. But I know of no reason for suspecting him of bad faith. All his amazing oracles can be sufficiently accounted for by the hypothesis of ignorance and overweening self-confidence.

One is, however, in a position to state that the information which he gives his readers about the opinions of Kant, Spinoza and Berkeley is exactly as valuable as what he tells them about the dates of composition and method of ecclesiastical selection of the four Gospels. The myth of the leaping Gospels he had picked up somewhere; but he has invented, out of his own head, the following myth about Immanuel Kant, which to students of philosophy will be equally amusing: —

The great majority of philosophers and theologians affirm, with Kant, that the moral world is quite independent of the physical, and is subject to very different laws; hence, a man's conscience, as the basis of his moral life, must also be quite independent of our scientific knowledge of the world, and must be based rather on his religious faith. On that theory the study of the moral world belongs to *practical* reason, while that of nature, or of the physical world, is referred to *pure* or theoretical reason. This unequivocal and conscious dualism of Kant's philosophy was its greatest defect; it has caused, and still causes, incalculable mischief. First of all the "critical Kant" had built up the splendid and marvellous palace of pure reason, and convincingly proved that the three great central dogmas of metaphysics — a personal God, free will, and the immortal soul — had no place whatever in it, and that no rational proof could be found of their reality. Afterwards, however, the "dogmatic Kant" superimposed on this true crystal palace of *pure* reason the glittering, ideal castle in the air of *practical* reason, in which three imposing church-naves were designed for the accommodation of those three great mystic divinities. When they had been put out at the front door by rational knowledge they returned by the back door under the guidance of irrational faith.[1]

This contrast between the critical and the dogmatic Kant, who in his capacity of dogmatist declared the moral world independent of the physical, and taught that conscience must be based on religious faith; who superimposed a glittering castle on top of a crystal palace, and stuck three church - naves (with back doors) into the former, is a precious addition to our knowledge of the philosopher of Königsberg. Not less delicious is the information as to the delimitation

[1] *Op. cit.*, chap. XIX, p. 123, 5th English edition.

of the spheres of pure and practical reason. It teaches
us at least one thing: that Professor Ernst Haeckel
has not the faintest glimmering of what Kant meant
by the pure reason and the distinction between it and
the practical reason. He obviously thinks that Kant
held successively — at different periods of his life —
the doctrine which got rid of God, freedom and immortality, and that which reinstated them. He does
not know that Kant's work was the destruction of
dogmas as dogmas — the eradication of the dogmatic
spirit and of the pseudo-rationalism of the older
metaphysics. While doing this, however, Kant retained the doctrines of God, freedom and immortality
with the different status of postulates of the practical
reason, or, as we should nowadays say, pragmatic assumptions. They are not demonstrable, but neither
are they disprovable; and (so Kant thought) they
serve to justify the intuitions of conscience. But
could there be a more outrageous perversion of truth
than the statement that Kant, of all people, taught
that conscience "must be based on religious faith"?
Kant, who in the plainest language taught the precise opposite — that religious faith must be based on
conscience — and declared that even God and Christ
can only be called good in so far as they correspond
to the ideal of perfection which is inherent in the
nature of man![1] Such passages enable one to understand the "burning shame" with which a real philo-

[1] *Vide* Kant, *Groundwork of the Metaphysic of Ethics*, chap. II.

sopher like Professor Paulsen observed the growing popularity of Haeckel's book.

Another amusing instance of our monistic philosopher's insight is afforded by his presentation of the doctrine of Spinoza, with which he professes to identify himself. Spinoza, as we know, held that the one universal reality manifests itself to us under the two aspects of mind and body. He held the theory of psycho-physical parallelism, from which, among other consequences, it follows that interaction between mind and brain is unthinkable. Professor Haeckel makes a parade of accepting this doctrine, but in the very sentence in which he does so, he reduces it to nonsense by identifying mind with physical force. And, as we have already seen, instead of standing consistently by his doctrine of psycho-physical parallelism (which would bar him out completely from denying immortality and the freedom of the will), he flops over to the notion of the *influxus physicus*. We have already [1] caught him declaring that the brain produces thought and consciousness. These elementary self-contradictions are, as we have said, not a proof of bad faith. His only fault ("and that is faults enough"!) is an incurable propensity to lay down the law about things of which he knows nothing, with even more than the excessive confidence he displays in expounding that branch of knowledge which is his special field.

[1] *Ante*, p. 88.

A man can believe either in psycho-physical parallelism or in physico-psychical interactionism, just as he can believe either that the earth is spherical or that it is flat; but it was reserved for this solver of the riddles of the universe at the end of the nineteenth century to hold both views simultaneously, without perceiving the difference between them.

Professor Haeckel's philosophic competence in discussing and solving his celebrated troupe of seven world-riddles is such as the foregoing might naturally lead us to anticipate. The riddles in question he takes over from du Bois - Reymond, who had enumerated them as follows: —

(1) The nature of matter and force.
(2) The origin of motion.
(3) The origin of life.
(4) The (apparently pre-ordained) orderly arrangement of nature.
(5) The origin of simple sensation and consciousness.
(6) Rational thought, and the origin of the cognate faculty, speech.
(7) The question of the freedom of the will.

Professor Haeckel, unabashed by these enigmas, which have baffled the mind of man from the beginning, and some at least of which will certainly continue until the end of time to baffle all who are capable of seeing the problems they involve, disposes of the whole septette by the ready and easy method of denying their existence: —

In my opinion, the three transcendental problems (1, 2 and 5) are settled by our conception of substance (*vide* chap. XII); the three which he [du Bois-Reymond] considers difficult, though soluble (3, 4 and 6) are decisively answered by our modern theory of evolution; the seventh and last, the freedom of the will, is not an object for critical, scientific inquiry at all, for it is a pure dogma, based on an illusion, and has no real existence.[1]

Ecclesia locuta est; causa finita est! The oracle of Jena has wrapped his pontifical mantle about him and delivered himself officially of the utterance *ex cathedrâ* which is henceforth to be binding on all the faithful. Yet stay! We have still one question left: what is "our conception of substance (*vide* chap. XII)"? With pardonable impatience we turn in quest of the revelation that "settles" the three transcendental problems of the nature of matter and force, the origin of motion, and the origin of simple sensation and consciousness. What do we find?

After telling us that, *in his opinion*, the "law of substance" is "the true and only cosmological law," Professor Haeckel proceeds to explain that this true and only law consists of two other laws. The striking resemblance of this threefold unity to the Athanasian Trinity cannot fail to impress itself upon reverent readers. We are offered one supreme and all-pervading law which does not itself relate to any data of experience whatever, but proceeds, apparently by

[1] *Op. cit.*, chap. I, p. 6, English translation, 5th edition.

eternal and transcendental self-generation, from two
of the presuppositions of empirical science. These are
the chemical law of the conservation of matter, and
the physical law of the conservation of energy. As
some hardy heretics still venture to dispute that these
are "essentially inseparable," our philosopher proceeds to furnish the "proof" of his thesis in the following paragraph: —

> The conviction that these two great cosmic theorems,
> the chemical law of the persistence of matter and the
> physical law of the persistence of force, are fundamentally
> one, is of the utmost importance in our monistic system.
> The two theories are just as intimately united as their
> objects — matter and force or energy. Indeed, this
> fundamental unity of the two laws is self-evident to
> many monistic scientists and philosophers, since they
> merely relate to two different aspects of one and the
> same object, the *cosmos*. But, however natural the
> thought may be, it is still very far from being generally
> accepted. It is stoutly contested by the entire dualistic
> philosophy, vitalistic biology, and parallelistic psy-
> chology; even, in fact, by a few (inconsistent) monists,
> who think they find a check to it in "consciousness,"
> in the higher mental activity of man, or in other phe-
> nomena of our "free mental life."
>
> For my part, I am convinced of the profound import-
> ance of the unifying "law of substance," as an expres-
> sion of the inseparable connection in reality of two laws
> which are only separated in conception.[1]

I assume that the foregoing quotation constitutes

[1] *Op. cit.*, chap. XII, p. 76, English translation, 5th edition.

the promised proof, because there is nothing else in
the entire chapter in the way of evidence for the thesis.
The merely lay mind will not be able, I am aware, to
find in the above passage any proof of this supreme
and all--pervading "law of substance" which Professor Haeckel has created out of nothing. It may be
unduly temerarious to analyze the dicta of infallible
authority, but, even at the risk of excommunication
from Dr. Haeckel's new monistic Church, one must
point out the utter baselessness of his claim. He has
invented, and promulgated without any evidence,
his wonderful new law, merely in order to buttress
the card-castle of his *a priori* philosophic structure.
The law is, he tells us, "of the utmost importance in
our monistic system." The ensuing assertion that the
two laws must be fundamentally one, "since they
merely relate to two different aspects of one and the
same object, the *cosmos*," is so breath-bereaving that
one turns hastily to the German original, to discover
whether Dr. Haeckel's meaning has not been unconsciously distorted by printer or translator. But no!
the "Hibernianism" is Haeckel's own:—"Beide
nur zwei verschiedene Seiten eines und desselben
Objekts, des 'Kosmos,' betreffen." Was ever such a
reason given, not merely for declaring the basic
identity of two natural laws, but for erecting the two
into three and then declaring that these three are one?
Will Professor Haeckel condescend to inform us of
any two or more natural laws which do *not* relate to

"different aspects of one and the same object, the cosmos"? On the same ground, we should be justified in affirming the fundamental unity of the law of gravitation and the American Tariff Act. Would anybody except Haeckel ever dream of implying that fifty different scientific generalizations may relate to fifty different worlds of experience? Instead of making his one universal fundamental law out of these two principles alone, he ought to have raked together all the laws that ever were formulated, and fused the lot into one comprehensive hypostatized abstraction, "without body, parts or passions."

And who are these wonderful dualistic philosophers, vitalistic biologists, parallelistic psychologists, and inconsistent monists who deny that the law of the conservation of energy and that of the indestructibility of matter are inseparably connected in reality? They do not exist; they are not there. Professor Haeckel has conjured them up out of his own superheated imagination.

Nor does the principle of the conservation of energy interfere with any psychological or philosophical theory of consciousness, except the untenable one to which Professor Haeckel, contradicting his claim to be a monist, has committed himself — that, namely, of interactionism. Of course, if a physical impulsion, traced from the outer world to the periphery of the human body, and thence by the afferent nerves to the brain, could there be shown to be suddenly metamorphosed into a state of consciousness, this would be equivalent, from the scientific point of view, to a miraculous disappearance or destruction of energy. But no such metamorphosis ever takes place, and no philosophy except materialism necessitates the hypothesis that it does. The whole muddle arises from Dr. Haeckel's preposterous identification of consciousness with physical force.

We have quoted above the paragraph in which Professor Haeckel declares that, of the seven world-riddles, six are already solved and the seventh is a pure illusion. But the passage cited was only an appendix to a series of pronouncements which are presumably to be understood as justifying it. Our philosopher tells us that "not only the three anthropistic dogmas, but many other notions of the dualistic philosophy and orthodox religion, are found to be untenable as soon as we regard them critically from the cosmological perspective of our monistic system." [1] This procession of polysyllables sounds impressive, but all it means is that the notions in question are found to be untenable the moment we arbitrarily adopt a set of unverifiable first principles with which they are incompatible. He then proceeds to formulate such assumptions. I have not space to quote them at length, but I will give a specimen, to show how this novel philosophy first takes for granted everything that it ought to prove, and then gets rid of rival philo-

[1] *Op. cit.*, chap. I, p. 5, English translation, 5th edition.

sophies by the simple expedient of showing their inconsistency with its own initial assumptions. Haeckel
begins in the following fashion: —

> (1) The universe, or the cosmos, is eternal, infinite
> and illimitable. (2) Its substance, with its two attri-
> butes (matter and energy), fills infinite space and is in
> eternal motion.

Here we have a new creation — a "substance"
which is neither matter nor energy nor yet spirit, but
to which matter and energy are both adjectival. And
this is "monism"!

Having thus set out with a huge bundle of self-
contradictory *petitiones principii*, the philosopher of
course has no hesitation or difficulty in deducing from
them his machine-made world of mere chemical and
physical causation, in which there is no room for consciousness or freedom. There never was a more glaring instance of the blunder of which Professor Bergson
accuses Herbert Spencer. Bergson's characterization
of Spencer's evolutionism is, indeed, a thousand times
truer of Haeckel's — viz., that it "consists in cutting
up present reality, already evolved, into little bits
no less evolved, and then recomposing it with these
fragments, thus positing in advance everything that
is to be explained." [1] It is thus that Haeckel gets
rid of the problem of the origin of the universe, by
saying that it "has no beginning and no end; it is

[1] *Creative Evolution*, English translation, Introduction, pp. xiii–
xiv.

eternity." And with respect to the origin of motion (which is really still as mysterious for us as it was for Aristotle) he calmly lays it down that "movement is as innate and original a property of substance *as is sensation.*"

The student unaccustomed to Professor Haeckel's peculiarities will naturally gasp at the assertion — made as though it were self-evident — that *sensation* is an innate and original property of substance. We ask him, however, to control his astonishment for the moment. The mystery will be explained a little later. He need not be impatient, for we are getting along pretty fast. We have already got the origin of the cosmos and the origin of motion cleared up in a couple of sentences. Now for the problem of the origin of life.

In chapter XIV, abiogenesis, or the development of life from non-life, is proclaimed, as it had been proclaimed earlier in the fourth chapter of Haeckel's "Evolution of Man." Again, in chapter XX of "Die Welträtsel," Haeckel tells us that the monera "arise by spontaneous generation from . . . inorganic nitrocarbonates." He is careful to restrict this miracle to "the *first development* of living protoplasm out of inorganic carbonates," [1] thus getting rid in advance of the embarrassing request that he should describe, or reproduce in his laboratory, the process by which living organisms are self-made out of dead matter.

[1] *Riddles*, chap. XIV, p. 91, English translation, 5th edition.

But in case anybody is not satisfied with this Topsy's explanation, our solver of world - riddles generously provides us with an alternative, according to which we are to suppose that the distinctive attributes of life — sensation and desire — are universal properties of all material substance whatsoever. He even talks [1] of the "psychology" of atoms, and informs us that "every shade of inclination, from complete indifference to the fiercest passion, is exemplified in the chemical relation of the various elements towards each other, just as we find in the psychology of man, and especially in the life of the sexes." A few sentences further on [2] we are informed that "even the *atom* is not without a rudimentary form of sensation and will, or, as it is better expressed, of feeling (*æsthesis*) and inclination (*tropesis*) — that is, a universal 'soul' of the simplest character."

Thus gently and seductively is the inquiring mind of man lulled to sleep in the arms of the all-embracing "law of substance." Benignly accommodating himself to the frailties of human nature, Professor Haeckel provides us with two distinct (and mutually destructive) versions of the origin of life. According to one of these, life begins of itself, by an inconceivable process, at an unknown time, and under unimaginable conditions. According to the other, it never begins at all, being coextensive with the fundamental properties of the eternal substance, which, as we have already learned,

[1] *Riddles*, p. 79, 5th English edition.   [2] *Ibid.*, p. 80.

fills infinite space and is without beginning or end
in time. It takes the giant mind of a Haeckel to
be able to hold both these antithetical beliefs simultaneously; but we of feebler powers are not constrained
to attempt so magnificent a feat. We can make a
Pascalian wager, and decide between the rival claim-
ants on our faith by the simple process of tossing up
a coin: heads, abiogenesis; tails, the soul of the atom!
We need not bother about the lack of evidence for the
winner, for both the doctrines have exactly the same
amount of evidence in their favour — and that is,
none at all.

Whoever has the mountain-moving faith to imagine
that these three "transcendental world-enigmas" are
solved by Professor Haeckel's *ipse dixit*, will find
nothing to baulk at in the subsequent explanation of
the " origin of consciousness and self-consciousness."
This, indeed, is but a reduplication of the thesis that
life "growed." With a stroke of his magic wand, Professor Haeckel transforms the brain of the ape into
the human brain, and then (as we have seen above)
points out in the latter the organs which *produce* consciousness. Here, then, are four of our seven world-
riddles compendiously settled out of hand; and who,
after this, will bother about such trifles as the apparently pre-ordained order of nature, the genesis of
rational thought and speech, and the freedom of the
will? Indeed, we learned at the outset that the so-
called problem of the freedom of the will has no right

to a place in the list of the "Welträtsel," being, in
fact, nothing but a pure dogma based on an illusion.
But even here we are not left without a supplement-
ary reassurance, furnished out of Professor Haeckel's
unbounded intimacy with all the secrets of existence.
He tells us (as usual, without condescending to argument) that

> The great struggle between the determinist and the
> indeterminist, between the opponent and the sustainer
> of the freedom of the will, has ended to-day, after more
> than two thousand years, completely in favour of the
> determinist. The human will has no more freedom than
> that of the higher animals, from which it differs only in
> degree, not in kind. . . . *We now know* that each act of
> the will is as fatally determined by the organization of
> the individual and as dependent on the momentary con-
> dition of his environment as every other psychic ac-
> tivity. The character of the inclination was determined
> long ago by *heredity* from parents and ancestors; the
> determination to each particular act is an instance of
> *adaptation* to the circumstances of the moment, wherein
> the strongest motive prevails, according to the laws
> which govern the statics of emotion.[1]

I have risked overloading my pages with quotations
in order to make convincingly apparent the amazing
levity with which Professor Haeckel substitutes af-
firmation for proof. But I would advise my reader also
to read the whole of his book. He will find thereby that
the samples I have chosen are strictly representative.

[1] *Riddles*, chap. VII, p. 47, English translation, 5th edition.

Our philosopher, without hesitation or misgiving, continually offers, as proved, statements which are as unproved and unprovable as those of the Athanasian Creed or the Westminster Confession. He also talks in romantic fashion about the world "obeying" the laws which he and his scientific predecessors have formulated. His much-trumpeted "law of substance" is not what ordinary thinkers understand a law to be — a generalization of the observed uniformities of experience; it is something imposed on the universe from without, and "obeyed" by "the innumerable bodies which are scattered about the space-filling ether." [1] For him, it is no figure of speech that the cosmos and its constituent parts are "by eternal laws of iron ruled." He is quite convinced that a natural law is itself a force or cause; and he does not escape from this ludicrous fallacy even when talking about an empirical law which he himself has formulated. One of his most useful contributions to the study of human race-history is the hypothesis that the development of the individual is a brief and rapid recapitulation of the entire evolution of the species. This statement, verified by many correspondences between embryonic development and the paleontological record of the history of the animal world, he calls the "biogenetic law." It means, to use his own words, that "ontogeny is a brief and condensed recapitulation of phylogeny." One would have expected Professor Haeckel to remember

[1] *Riddles*, chap. I, p. 5, English translation, 5th edition.

that such a law — even if universally verified, which it is not — would be merely a statement of the fact *that* certain phenomena happen. Yet over and over again, in his "Anthropogenie," he makes this fact the cause of itself, and talks of things happening "in virtue of the biogenetic law." At the close of this book he writes: —

> There remains only the ... monistic conception, according to which the human soul is, like any other animal soul, a function of the central nervous system, and develops in inseparable connection therewith. We see this *ontogenetically* in every child. The biogenetic law compels us to affirm it *phylogenetically*.[1]

But how can his own home-made law "compel" him to affirm anything of the sort apart from experience, seeing that his law is only a generalization of his experience? Unless the thesis that the soul is a function of the nervous system (whatever that may mean) can be proved without invoking his biogenetic principle — or, conversely, if the facts are inferred from the principle and not the principle from the facts — his "law" has no claim to be so called, even in the strictly limited scientific meaning of the term.

The bundle of world-riddles which Professor Haeckel solves by denying their existence, are not necessarily, in all cases, inherently insoluble. A truly scientific and philosophical procedure may, at all events, in

[1] *Evolution of Man* (English translation of *Anthropogenie*), popular edition, 1906, p. 355.

future throw much more light upon them than we have to-day. It is, for example, not inconceivable that we may one day be able to define conditions under which a non-biogenetic appearance of life would take place. It is not entirely unthinkable that we may some day learn whether the physical universe did or did not have a beginning in time, and whether, if so, its parts were originally in motion or not. We cannot be Pyrrhonists; but it is incumbent upon us to see that we really know what we think we know, and not to deceive ourselves, or be deceived by others, into imagining that we know a host of things about which we really know nothing.

Now, what Professor Haeckel offers us as proved is a series of affirmations, which must either be based on a supernatural revelation, vouchsafed exclusively to himself, or else mere speculations on the secrets of the universe. Who told him that the universe is eternal, infinite and illimitable? What does he *know* (hypotheses apart) of an "infinite space," whether distinct or not from the "substance" which fills it? What basis has he for his doctrine of abiogenesis, except the fact that his *a priori* dogmas make him wish to find it true? And in regard to the freedom of the will, how does he know that every act of will is fatally determined? If he had ever read Bergson's "Time and Free Will" [1] he would have seen that the great

[1] This book, under its French title (*Essai sur les Données immédiates de la Conscience*), was published many years before *The Riddles of*

struggle between the opponent and the sustainer of
the freedom of the will is by no means settled in favour
of the former. He would have learned, on the contrary,
that it is still possible for a philosopher of high scientific competence to dispute the very presuppositions of
the mechanical-determinist argument. What Bergson
questions (and in my opinion rightly) is whether the
spatial categories of quantity, number and magnitude
can legitimately be applied to any states of consciousness — even to sensations. No doubt the mind too
has its uniformities; but, though these be determinate,
they nevertheless manifest a determinism *sui generis*,
whose sequences are not, and never will be, measur-
able and predictable by the same standards and instruments as those of physical nature.

Let us now return to the enlightening and inspiring
conclusion as to the nature and potentialities of man
which Haeckel deduces from his body of dogmas about
the universe in general. We have seen that he makes
mind the product and effect of matter. Without its
material substratum it cannot exist, and our philosopher accordingly denies dogmatically the immortality
of the soul.[1] Body, therefore, is the only reality, and

the Universe was written. But evidently Haeckel has never heard of
Bergson. This perhaps is the less to be wondered at, seeing that a
recent disciple of Haeckel, Mr. Hugh S. R. Elliot, has written a volume on *Modern Science and the Illusions of Professor Bergson*, without
having ever read *Time and Free Will*.

[1] "These inquiries, which might be supplemented by many other
results of modern science, prove the old dogma of the immortality of
the soul to be absolutely untenable." (English translation, 5th edition, p. 73.) It is needless to add that in the whole of Haeckel's

man is but a momentary phenomenon in the eternal flux of things, impotent and transient as foam-flakes on the waves. We have quoted above (p. 88) Haeckel's conclusion that humanity, being but a special and temporary form of matter and force, has "no more value for the universe at large than the ant, the fly of a summer's day," and all the rest of it.

But what, in such a philosophy, can possibly be the meaning of the phrase, "value for the universe at large"? This wonderful philosopher, having got rid of the idea of any purpose in the world, now falls back upon language which can only mean that, after all, there *is* a purpose in things. How can anything whatever be of "value" to such a universe as he has evolved from the abysses of his imagination? No words could express the depths of Professor Haeckel's contempt for any theologian who should talk about value to the universe — thereby implying that the universe as a whole has ends and purposes in view. The truth is that the category of value has meaning and use for man alone. The question is not so much what we are worth to the universe, but what the universe is worth to us.

It is needless, at this stage, to add that the central problem of philosophy, which is that of the relation

eleventh chapter, entitled "The Immortality of the Soul," nothing whatever is adduced to "prove" this comprehensive negative. Apart from the preliminary assumption that the soul is something which the body secretes, the physiological and other facts which he sets forth give no support to his conclusion.

of thought to its object, has not only not been solved, but has never even been perceived by Professor Haeckel. He speaks of "the absurd idealism" of Berkeley's thesis that the essence of bodies is in their perception. Rushing in, as usual, where angels might fear to tread, he serenely lays it down that the thesis should be corrected to read as follows: —

> Bodies are only ideas for my personal consciousness; their existence is just as real as that of my organs of thought, the ganglionic cells in the grey bed of my brain, which receive the impress of bodies on my sense-organs, and form those ideas by association of the impressions.[1]

It has never occurred to him that these wonderful "organs of thought" are themselves only ideas — only items in consciousness. Yet the epiphenomenon which, according to Haeckel, they produce, is the only reality he or anybody else knows immediately and unquestionably. In the same confident fashion, he dismisses Kant's thesis of the transcendental ideality of time and space, by saying that this applies only to the subjective side of the problem, and demanding that we should recognize the equal validity of the objective side. And by "objective" he does not mean what another philosopher would mean — namely, that these transcendentally ideal forms of perception are valid not only for the individual but for conscious-

[1] *Riddles*, chap. XIII, p. 87, English translation, 5th edition. Note the repetition of the unintelligible dogma that the cells of the brain "form ideas."

ness in general. No; what he means is that they exist independently of any consciousness; that, like the material world of his imagination, they are prior to and altogether independent of mind. And he even goes on to say, in a transport of sublime absurdity, that "the reality of time and space is now fully established by that expansion of our philosophy which we owe to the law of substance, and to our monistic cosmogony." That is to say, his evolutionary mythology succeeds in proving the fundamental forms of rationality, which are presupposed in every single step by which the mind advances to its formulation! It is a pity he has never read the metaphysical portions of Green's "Prolegomena to Ethics." His comments on that book would have been as funny as his remarks on Kant and Berkeley.

But it is wearisome to heap up the refutation of a creed so manifestly baseless. As Paulsen said, it is infallibility which speaks to us in Haeckel's pages; and only those who are willing to accept a new Pope at his own valuation will be imposed upon by one who seeks to hide beneath a cloud of new and ugly words the beggarly poverty of his thought. Our interest in him and his pronouncements arises merely from the fact that over a million human beings have purchased his work, and thousands of them, in every modern nation, actually mistake him for a scientific philosopher, a revealer of new truths, as well as the destroyer of a number of superstitions.

Now, what are likely to be the moral effects of this new Calvinism of Haeckel's, in which original sin is rebaptized heredity and predestination labelled determinism, and which has no occasion for a hell after death only because it has provided such an efficient substitute in this life, in the shape of man's utter impotence, and the illusoriness of his spiritual aspirations?

One need not anticipate that the diffusion of this new brand of materialism is likely to bring about any widespread moral deterioration; and this for two reasons. The first is that, as we have noted before, it is no new thing for the Western world to be materialistic; *its* Christianity has always been so. The second reason is that, as Fichte said, a man's character is not so much determined by his philosophy as is his philosophy by his character.[1] In other words, it is because we have always been trained to consider the world of the senses as more real than the world of the spirit, and because even our religion has lost sight of spiritual realities through its obsession by the bodily symbols which it has substituted for them, that our age is so completely predisposed to fall a prey to teachers of Haeckel's calibre. His mechanical determinism is truly a doctrine of despair; yet it is no more so than the predestinationism of St. Augustine and Calvin. Both views reduce man's personality to a shadow, a mere

[1] "Was für eine Philosophie man wähle, hängt davon ab, was für ein Mensch man ist. Denn die Philosophie ist kein toter Hausrat, den man an- und ablegen konnte, sondern sie ist beseelt durch die Seele des Menschen, der sie hat."

pale reflection of outward things, having no force in itself, and lost in illusion when it dreams of resisting its environment.

What is needed in the modern world is that we should make a clean sweep of both types of fatalism — the theological and the pseudo-scientific alike. If Fichte be right, a philosophic reform cannot precede, but must advance step for step with, a moral and spiritual reawakening. We may thus return to the sense that Plato had, that ideas and ideals are real with a primary reality — more real than the sun and the stars and the many-coloured panorama of the outward world. Only this truth can justify our intuitive revulsion from the money-worship and the luxury-worship which, in our time more than ever before, are eating into the souls of nations. America to-day is palsied by the moral scepticism which expresses itself in the conviction that every man has his cash price, and is a fool if he does not make it a high one. Such a standard of values turns life into dust and ashes. In every case of national ruin which history has preserved to us, it was this practical materialism and ethical scepticism which ultimately caused the collapse, by producing the conditions which made it inevitable. If present-day civilization dies, it will die of these idolatries, to which Professor Haeckel's sham philosophy is the appropriate theoretical counterpart. We must go back to the ancient sense that the true values of life lie in goods which cannot even be formulated in materialistic terms: in fraternity and justice, in honour and magnanimity, in

> Truth and life-lightening Duty,
> Love without crown or sword,
> That by his might and godhead makes man god and lord.

To many minds to-day the sense of uncertainty, the attitude of suspended judgment towards the problems of the world, is so intensely painful that any sort of a ready-made answer to the soul's questions is preferable to it. This it is which accounts for the survival of orthodox theology, as well as for the popularity of Haeckel's new Calvinism, both of which, to quote the words of Mr. F. H. Bradley, "vanish like ghosts before the breath of free sceptical inquiry." But the pain which people feel, in the presence of a mystery acknowledged to be such, is due to inadequate reflection on the implications of man's moral nature, and to the false training of fifteen hundred years of ecclesiastical dogmatism, with its insistence that a complete account of the origin and destiny of the universe and of the human soul is a necessary pre-condition of righteousness. I will not repeat what in the preceding chapter I have said of mysticism and of its opposition to the certitude of orthodoxy. Suffice it to say that the truly inspiring as well as the truly wise attitude towards life is neither that of the old nor the new dogmatist, to whom nothing is unknown, and for whom life can conceal no surprises. It is rather that of the old adventurers, who set sail in their feeble boats across the un-

charted seas, not knowing whether even the sequences
of nature to which they were accustomed might not
be replaced by others in the unknown lands towards
which they journeyed. It is this sense of the unex-
hausted possibilities of life which we regain through a
sceptical re-examination, resulting in rejection, of the
materialistic fairy-tales of the priests of theology and
of physical science. There is a zest and a charm in the
challenging unknown which no mechanistic or finalistic
theory can ever impart. It lies in the sense that we in
part create the future into which we are ever pressing. We therefore can stand towards it in the temper
of the old mariners, whose adventurous exultation is
so wonderfully conveyed in the lines of Coleridge: —

> The fair breeze blew, the white foam flew,
>   The furrow followed free;
> We were the first that ever burst
>   Into that silent sea.

What may be the end of humanity's quest for
self-realization we neither know nor care to know.
Whether, apart from us, the world is animated by a
purpose, whether mind can exist apart from body or
body apart from mind, whether this mortal shall put
on immortality — all these are idle questions; questions that the mystic never cares to put. His joy in
life and action is self-justifying. He is contemptuous
of the answers of materialism to the enigmas of the
world, and equally contemptuous of those of orthodox
theology. He resents their irrelevance, as well as their

intellectual futility. For him, the very charm of life lies in its inscrutability. He loves too much the presence of the eternal Questioner to desire its dethronement. He is inspired and impelled to highest achievement not only by the invincible certainties of immediate ethical experience, but also by the sense of

> The sweet strange mystery
> Of what beyond these things may lie,
> And yet remains unseen.

NOTE

The English translations of the two most popular of Haeckel's works, "The Riddles of the Universe" and "The Evolution of Man," are issued by the Rationalist Press Association in London, of which the present writer is a member. This circumstance may seem to the reader of the foregoing chapter to call for some explanation. My reply to the criticism which I anticipate is that in my attack upon Haeckel I have been, as I trust I am throughout this book, rigidly loyal both to the letter and to the spirit of Rationalism, as officially defined by the Association in the following words: "The mental attitude which unreservedly accepts the supremacy of reason, and aims at establishing a system of philosophy and ethics verifiable by experience and independent of all arbitrary assumptions or authority."

Thus Rationalists are *ipso facto* freethinkers. The Association is, of course, not responsible for everything written by the authors whose works it publishes. It has erred, in my judgment, by printing and circulating the writings of Professor Haeckel, whose so-called system of philosophy is not verifiable by experience, is a mass of arbitrary assumptions, and is accepted by most of his devotees merely on the authority of its author. But for this error the Association has splendidly compensated by the admirable selection of works of real thinkers which it has issued to the public at the cheapest possible rates. By bringing out the works of such writers as Lecky, Huxley, Darwin, Hume, Matthew Arnold, John Stuart Mill, and many others, at twelve cents a volume, it has rendered an enormous service to popular thought and culture — a service which it is devoutly to be wished that some public-spirited body would undertake in the United States.

CHAPTER IV

SIR OLIVER LODGE AND THE EVIDENCE FOR
IMMORTALITY

THE annual Presidential Address to the British Association for the Advancement of Science is one of the institutions of England, an institution which has already gathered around it a distinguished tradition. Everybody has read or heard of the address of Professor Tyndall at Belfast in 1878, in which he made for science the tremendous claim that it would wrest from theology the whole field of human knowledge. The tradition thus set, marking as it did an epoch in that "warfare between science and theology" for which the nineteenth century is memorable, has been well sustained by the majority of the addresses from the Association's presidential chair which have followed.

It is interesting to compare the discourse on "Continuity" delivered in 1913 by Sir Oliver Lodge with the utterance in the previous year of Sir Ernest Schaefer. The latter is a biologist of the extreme materialistic type, and the burden of his discourse was that all life, including the highest mental processes of mankind, is reducible to the interaction of atoms of matter, according to unvarying chemical laws. He closed his address by affirming that death is purely and simply a physiological process, and by expressing a weird sort of hope that the recognition of this fact will reconcile man to dissolution more than any other thought has been able to do.

The selection of Sir Oliver Lodge to succeed Sir Ernest Schaefer looks suspiciously like a conspiracy. For many years Sir Oliver has been almost as notorious as a devotee of psychical research as he has been justly famous as a physicist. He has repeatedly, in book after book and in speech after speech, declared himself a believer in human immortality. One cannot say, of course, that the choice of him under these special circumstances was a conscious conspiracy; but there is sufficient evidence of purpose in the matter to justify an argument for design on the part of any belated survivor of the school of Paley.

One welcomes, to begin with, Sir Oliver Lodge's denunciation of the dogmatism of the materialistic school. Direct controversy in a Presidential Address to the British Association is naturally excluded by the traditions of good form associated with the post, but Sir Oliver Lodge gets as near to it as it is possible for a man to do, without actually mentioning names. His whole discourse, more especially in its closing paragraphs, is a direct refutation of the position taken by his predecessor, and of the popular materialism associated in the public mind with the writings of Professor Ernst Haeckel. Several years ago Sir Oliver Lodge wrote a book called "Life and Matter," which was a critical examination of Haeckel's "Riddles of the Universe," and in his Presidential Address he repeats, in summary form, the conclusions there advanced.

In so far as Sir Oliver Lodge rebukes the confident dogmatic denials of the materialistic biologists, I am heartily at one with him; but unfortunately he himself seems to fall into a counter-dogmatism which goes as far beyond evidence and experience as the materialistic position falls short of them. "Science," he says, "cannot make comprehensive denials." "It is always extremely difficult to deny *anything* of a general character, since evidence in its favour may be only hidden and not forthcoming." He ought to recognize, however, that, from the scientific point of view, it is quite as illegitimate to make comprehensive assertions in the absence of sufficient verified evidence.

It may be convenient to outline one's own position with regard to the belief in immortality before discussing that of Sir Oliver Lodge. For myself, when the question is put to me, "If a man die, shall he live again?" I am constrained to answer that, for all we know, it is perfectly possible. Nothing that I have met with in the literature of biology or any other science seems to give the slightest weight to the confident and dogmatic denials of human immortality which one finds in the writings of men like Haeckel. I say this in full consciousness of the strength of the case set up in 1912 by Sir Ernest Schaefer. Nay, I am willing to go beyond the evidence which the materialistic school is at present in a position to adduce. Let us assume that biology will at last succeed in proving its contention that life arose originally from non-living matter. Let the familiar dictum of Harvey, "Omne vivum ex vivo," be completely disproved. Let the actual process by which the first organisms were engendered by natural development from inorganic matter be reproduced in the laboratory. Then let it further be demonstrated that every possible activity of the human mind at its highest level is coincident with and correlative to some definitely assignable physical change. It still will not be proved, or provable, that mental and psychic activity are impossible apart from the functioning of that special material instrument which we call the human body.

For the weakness of the materialistic case is that it ignores throughout the only vital consideration. It denies the reality of that one fact which we know directly and at first hand. It reduces consciousness to an illusion, or, to use its ponderous term, an epiphenomenon. Consciousness is for this school an accidental by-product of physical functioning, hard to account for, but not to be permitted to disturb in the least our physical calculations and conclusions.

Now, the unanswerable argument, as it seems to me, which one must address to the materialists is that it is this epiphenomenon, this intractable fraction, this residual by-product of the processes that science describes, which is our one and only guarantee for the validity of all our other knowledge. Our very belief in the existence of our own bodies, and in the external world of which they are a part, is dependent upon, and presupposes, complete confidence in the validity of the testimony of consciousness. If mind be unreal, or real with only a secondary degree of reality, then the outer world in which we believe on the testimony of mind is reduced to the level of hallucination. If we cannot trust our only direct experience, our own consciousness, then we are compelled to distrust the very argument by which materialistic science seeks to invalidate our belief in the reality of consciousness. For that argument presupposes the thing it seeks to disprove. This is what Schopenhauer meant when he declared that it was "the absurd undertaking of materialism to derive the subject from the object."

We find ourselves in a world of sights and sounds, of touch, taste and smell. Yet all these sensations, and the regularities of co-existence and sequence to which they testify, are in fact presented to us only as modifications of our consciousness. Constrained as we are to believe in some sort in the reality of this world of sense-impressions, we are *ipso facto* constrained to ascribe a prior and deeper reality to our own percipient selfhood. This is the indubitable fact which has led philosophers like Berkeley to declare that the existence of the physical universe consists wholly in the fact that it is perceived or perceivable.

The materialist who is able and willing to follow this

argument will, of course, be ready with his reply. Your contention, he will say, is all very well, but you cannot deny that the body, the brain and the nervous system are absolutely necessary to consciousness. I answer that, so far as experience goes, we have no right to say more than that this physical substratum is necessary to the *manifestation of consciousness to other conscious agents similarly conditioned*. We meet with no disclosure of the existence of consciousness, no evidence of the presence or activity of mind, except in conjunction with a material body. We are, therefore, entitled to say that, so far as experience goes, mind and body are two aspects of a unity. But this does not justify us in saying that consciousness cannot exist independently of the special physical machinery with which alone we find it associated; and *a fortiori* we cannot deny that it might manifest itself in activities conditioned by other machinery than that with which we are at present acquainted.

The argument used by Professor James, in his Ingersoll Lecture on "Human Immortality," is thus far unanswered and seems unanswerable from the materialistic standpoint. The brain, says the materialist, is the organ of mind. For every act of consciousness there is presumably, and in some cases assignably, a corresponding physiological modification. Agreed, says Professor James; we accept the position that the brain is the organ of mind. But such a statement is susceptible of at least two interpretations. The organ may either produce that of which it is the instrument, or its function may be limited to that of transmission. In our experience, for example, electricity is associated with things like batteries, dynamos and wires. The wire is the organ of the electric current. Without the wire (the argument, of course, was formulated before the days of wireless, but ethereal vibrations will answer its purpose just as well) there could be no manifestation of electricity. But nobody supposes that the wire produces that of which it is the organ, or that the electricity ceases to exist when the wire is disconnected or destroyed. It ceases, indeed, to manifest itself to us; but we know that this absence of manifestation is not identical with non-existence. And so, for all we know, it may be with mind. Its manifestation to us is dependent upon the efficient functioning of those particular items in consciousness which we call the brain and nervous system. But nothing in our experience, scientific or otherwise, entitles us to say that it could not exist apart from its organ, or that it might not, under other conditions and to other conscious agents, be manifested through an organ of different nature. Nor is it yet by any means demonstrated that the connection between brain and mind is of the nature of a complete parallelism. The ingenious hypothesis of M. Bergson, that the brain acts only as a screen, to exclude from consciousness the vast mass of psychic elements that are always pressing against it and admit only those that are serviceable at the moment, seems at least no less consistent with the ascertained facts than the psycho-physical parallelism of Fechner and Paulsen.[1]

One must therefore dismiss the materialistic denial of immortality as a piece of dogmatism, which is as unprovable as any of the theological dogmas which the materialistic school rejects. It is an expression of philosophic incompetence, and, in general, of a personal predilection in favour of the negative conclusion. Sir Oliver Lodge makes admirably the point that we have to guard against personal predilection in the negative direction as well as in the affirmative. We all know how theological polemics have been vitiated by the fact that the controversialist's conclusion visibly comes before his premises. His process of reasoning is introduced only to justify a foregone conclusion; his predilection is the parent of his argument. This psychological tendency has to be borne in mind when we are dealing with the arguments of those who deny theological positions, as well as of those who affirm them.

But the greatest error of Sir Oliver Lodge seems to consist in the fact that he confuses the abstractly possible with the actual. He has overlooked a principle of reasoning formulated nearly two hundred years ago by that keenest of theologians, Bishop Butler. In

[1] Bergson's doctrine, set forth in his *Matter and Memory*, and in his discourse on *Dreams*, seems more consistent than any other extant hypothesis with the facts of dream-life and of abnormal psychology as recently set forth by Freud. See the latter's *Interpretation of Dreams* and *Psychopathology of Everyday Life*. (English translations by Brill, published by Macmillan & Co.)

Butler's "Analogy of Religion" we find it laid down, with that clear precision which marks the born thinker, that "Suppositions are not to be looked on as true, because not incredible." This is what Sir Oliver Lodge forgets. He stands as the advocate, I will not say of a new superstition, but at all events of a new *Aberglaube* — a belief that exceeds any available evidence. He is as unwarrantably confident in his affirmations as the materialist in his denials. "The facts," he says, "have convinced me that memory and affection are not limited to that association with matter by which alone they can manifest themselves here and now, and that personality persists beyond bodily death." My contention is that Sir Oliver Lodge is not entitled, logically or scientifically, even to this attitude of personal conviction. The true position, in view of our present knowledge, is one of suspended judgment. The finest result of a scientific training is the production of that rigorous standard of accuracy, which enables a man to know at once when he does not know, and prevents him from allowing any predilection to force him a single inch in the direction of unwarranted assertion.

It is not inconceivable, for example, that in a year from now I may inherit or acquire a fortune of a million dollars. Anybody who affirmed this to be impossible would thereby write himself down a pedantic dogmatist. But I in my turn should be extremely foolish if I were to treat this bare possibility as a certainty or even a probability. The path of prudence for me is to assume that a year hence I shall be as dependent for my livelihood on my exertions as I am to-day. And so it is with the question of a life after death. To rush from the bare abstract possibility to a belief in the actuality of such a future is both logically and morally unjustifiable.

Let us examine one of many instances of the way in which Sir Oliver Lodge makes this illicit leap. In his book entitled "The Substance of Faith Allied with Science," which is drawn up in the form of a catechism, we find on page 20 the following Question and Answer: —

Question: Are there any beings higher in the scale of existence than man?

Answer: Man is the highest of the dwellers on the planet Earth, but the Earth is only one of many planets warmed by the sun, and the sun is only one of a myriad of similar suns, which are so far off that we barely see them and group them indiscriminately as stars. *We may reasonably conjecture* that in some of the innumerable worlds circling round those distant suns *there must be* beings far higher in the scale of existence than ourselves; indeed, we have no knowledge which enables us to assert the absence of intelligence anywhere.[1]

The jump from "conjecture" to "must" illustrates vividly the process by which Sir Oliver Lodge has arrived at his belief in man's survival of death. If it is a matter of conjecture whether other worlds than ours

[1] Italics mine.

are inhabited by intelligent beings, we obviously have
no right to say that such beings "must" exist. If the
evidence forces us to use the word "must," then the
word "conjecture" is grotesquely inapplicable. Sir
Oliver Lodge's habit of thought seems invariably to
be that if we have no knowledge which enables us
to affirm the *absence* of intelligence, we are entitled to
affirm its presence. Logic demands, however, the
admission that we have no knowledge which enables
us to assert the *presence* of intelligence anywhere save
on earth. This was fully admitted, and indeed contended, by a thinker as eminent in science as Sir Oliver
Lodge, and, as it happens, not less eminent also as a
spiritist: the late Alfred Russel Wallace. The thesis
of his recent book on "Man's Place in the Universe"
is that the earth alone, of all the worlds observable
by us, is fitted to be the abode of intelligent organisms. Man as a rational creature, he maintains, stands
solitary in the universe. The basis of his argument is
that only on the earth does there exist the unique as-
semblage of circumstances necessary for the existence
of living and intelligent beings. That combination of
the temperature necessary to life with a breathable
atmosphere and an adequate supply of fresh water,
does not exist in any other star or planet discernible
through the instruments of astronomy. It well may
be that Dr. Wallace went too far in his inferences
from the evidence on this point. It is the kind of reasoning which made some of the ancients pronounce

the existence of antipodes impossible, and made
Locke's Indian prince scout the idea that water in
England became solid in winter. I am concerned only
to show that Sir Oliver Lodge's belief in intelligences
higher than man is indeed a bare conjecture, which
he is not entitled to speak of as a belief necessitated
by evidence.

Let us turn now to a brief consideration of the
alleged facts which have convinced this distinguished
man of science that death is only an incident in the
continuous life of man. The reader is presumably
familiar with the kind of evidence collected by the
Society for Psychical Research and published in its
"Transactions," as well as in books like Sir Oliver
Lodge's "Survival of Man," Myers's "Human Personality," the book called "Phantasms of the Living,"
and in spiritualistic literature generally. In Sir Oliver
Lodge's book we find that much of the evidence adduced, even if it were validated in detail, would give
no support to faith in survival. The greater part of his
volume consists of evidence for telepathy and for automatic writing. If telepathy were proved, it would only
demonstrate that the living human mind, associated
with a body, possesses powers transcending those
hitherto allowed for in our philosophy. If a message
can be conveyed from Jones's mind to Brown's, apart
from the channels of communication hitherto recognized, that only proves that Jones, "whilst this machine
is to him," is able to exercise a wider activity than we

had supposed. It does not in the least demonstrate that his mind will survive his body. Indeed, the most scientific of the experimenters have maintained that there is a physical medium of communication, consisting of ethereal vibrations set going by brain activity, in all cases of telepathy. If this be so, then such communication is proved to be as truly dependent on the brain as speech is.

In the same way, the process of automatic writing is evidence only of hitherto unsuspected sub-conscious powers in the writer. The script may indeed purport to contain messages from other minds, but we are clearly not entitled scientifically to postulate the presence of any mentality other than that of the writer. The cases of secondary and tertiary personality, familiar to abnormal psychology, show how unsuspectedly wide is the range of possible mental activity; and the complete forgetfulness which the patient in one stage shows of his conscious activities in another proves how possible it is for the automatic writer to give, in perfect good faith, what purport to be messages from the dead, while they are in fact only the outcroppings of strata of his own personality which usually lie below the threshold of consciousness.

The case is the same with the argument from apparitions. We are offered a multitude of instances in which the dying have appeared, apparently in physical form, to friends at a distance. Let us set aside all question of the accuracy of the records and of the subjectivity of the visions, and assume, for the purpose of our argument, that the stories are in all cases true. What follows? No argument whatever for survival; only the fact that one living human being can, under unusual circumstances, perceive a phantasm of another *equally living* human being. It is not asserted that the phantasms are those of persons already dead; they are only those of persons about to die. Their message is, *Morituri salutamus*. It is perfectly conceivable that the imminence of death may be the specific condition for the occurrence of such experiences; but we are not entitled on the basis of such evidence to conclude that the dying person survives his physical dissolution.

The greatest stronghold, however, of the belief in survival is the multitudinous testimony of the séance-room. But this again is vitiated for scientific purposes by the fact that we do not know the limits either of the mind or body of the living human being. Even physically, we are ignorant of the nether limit, so to speak, of our potentialities. Doctors assure us that the undiscoverable causes of many diseases are in all probability ultra-microscopic, — the effects, that is, of organisms which are too small to be made visible, and which give no traceable reaction to the most delicate tests which science has thus far been able to devise. If this be true of the body, how much more true is it of our mental and psychic activities.

Let us apply this criterion to the mass of mediumistic communications, slate-writings and alleged letters from the spirit world, which for many people constitute the basis of belief in personal survival. Here again we will set aside all question of fraud, and leave out of consideration the very important problem as to the competence of the investigators. Mr. Sludge, we know, has had hosts of imitators, but we will forget them for the moment. Assuming both perfect good faith in the medium and scientific competence in the witnesses, what is the value of the evidence adduced? The answer is that the only thing clearly testified to is an unaccustomed and unclassifiable activity on the part of the medium himself. Suppose he speaks with another voice and discloses so novel a context of knowledge and experience as to seem a wholly different person from his normal self. There is still no proof of the presence of an independent individuality. The verification offered for these communications is generally the statement that somebody present knows the facts involved. The medium is ostensibly controlled, let us say, by the spirit of Mr. Gladstone. He talks in Gladstone's person and discloses, we will assume, facts which occurred in Gladstone's experience but not in that of the medium in his primary personality. Such facts can only be verified if some one or more of the observers are acquainted with them. But in this case why should not the source of the medium's knowledge be precisely the consciousness or sub-consciousness of the observer who knows the facts? If telepathy be a reality, how do we know that the medium is not unconsciously tapping the mind of the observer and constructing his narrative from hints so obtained?

It may be urged that telepathy is not a demonstrated fact; but "secondary personality" is demonstrated; and science and logic constrain us to consider both as possible explanations before resorting to the unnecessary multiplication of entities involved in the spiritistic hypothesis.

Most of us, I suppose, are familiar with that queer experience of reminiscence, which consists in finding oneself in a company where one has never been before, and yet having a sudden, convincing premonition of what is next to be said or done. This experience is a common one. Dickens, among others, testifies to it; and it has more than once happened to myself. Conversing with friends or strangers, sitting on a committee, or conducting a discussion on one of my own lectures, it has many times been my fate to feel an intuitive certainty as to what would be said next; and, so far as I can recall, I have never been mistaken in my anticipation. The "daimon" seems to know his business. How is this to be explained? We do not know; but the simplest hypothesis seems to be that of an unclassified activity of mind which effects a communication more rapid than that of the normal channels, and therefore anticipates the slower action of the organs of speech. Such an hypothesis would account for a vast percentage of the alleged facts from which spiritists infer the presence of discarnate intelligence.

And now, conceding for the sake of argument that man's survival could be proved, there are three criticisms to be passed, which seem almost invariably to be overlooked by believers like Sir Oliver Lodge.

The first of these is that the proof of *survival* is a totally different thing from the proof of *immortality*. Sir Oliver Lodge is always talking of immortality, and that in a fashion which leads us to suppose that he considers it synonymous with survival. This is another of the illicit leaps in logic which seem to prove that, for him too, the conclusion antedates the premises. If the argument from analogy is good for anything, it would lead us to suppose that a life after death will be transient, like our bodily life on earth. The most convinced spiritualist of them all is forced to concede that one of the conditions of that after-life is the attainment of a new instrument, material or "ethereal," analogous to, though possibly finer and more delicate than, the human body. If this be so, how can we suppose that such an instrument is not subject to a slow attrition akin to that which in time wears out our present vehicle of spiritual communication? Since, then, life here is temporary, an after-life may be no less so; and a proof of survival would leave us as far off as ever from a proof of immortality.

A second unwarrantable assumption made by many believers in an after-life is that the establishment of such a life would be a verification of the dogmas of orthodox Christianity. Here, however, we need to be reminded of another of the utterances of the great theologian whom I have already quoted. "A proof," says Bishop Butler, "even a demonstrative one, of a future life would not be a proof of religion." (By religion, of course, he means orthodox Christian theology.) "For, that we are to live hereafter is just as reconcilable with the scheme of atheism, and as well to be accounted for by it, as that we are now alive is." In other words, if a naturalistic philosophy can account for our existence here and now, without the hypothesis of a superhuman personal God, or of miraculous intervention in the economy of nature, the same philosophy could equally well account for mental and psychical existence in conditions totally different from those of our present life. The apologist of theology, therefore, must not think that the séance-room is ever going to furnish a buttress for its assumptions.

The third criticism which one must make, upon such an after-life as would be in store for men if we were compelled to believe in Sir Oliver Lodge's evidence, is perhaps the most important of all. Sir Oliver and his co-believers invariably assume that the after-life must be a far finer, grander and nobler state of being than our present existence. They speak of it with an enthusiasm akin to that displayed by believers in Christian orthodoxy in their pictures of heaven. But if we ask the grounds for this assumption, we find that there are none. We have here the proof that the so-called scientific believers in immortality are in reality not scientific at all. They believe in an *a priori* theory, and they overlook the contradictions to that theory which lie on the face of the very evidence which they themselves adduce. For if we are to believe in the messages that come from that other world, we shall be forced to conclude that the human spirit after death undergoes a most startling and disheartening deterioration in quality and capacity. I have read masses of these alleged communications, purporting to emanate from the greatest minds that have illuminated the pathway of history, and they seem (to put it mildly) more like the babblings of imbecility than the utterances of genius. Among these messages have been letters from F. W. H. Myers, one of the finest writers, as well as one of the noblest souls, of the nineteenth century. Being vouchsafed in America, these utterances and epistles have been full of Americanisms — surely a startling development in Myers's use of the English language. They have also been full of errors of grammar for which a sixth-form schoolboy would incur merited chastisement. And, for the rest, they have been a tissue of banalities which might have emanated from any one of a thousand hopelessly commonplace people, but which never could have been uttered by a profound thinker and a fine scholar like Mr. Myers. The same is true of the alleged messages from a hundred great minds. In a collection of such documents, published in London in 1912 by Admiral Moore,[1] we find communications

[1] *Glimpses of the Next State: the Education of an Agnostic.* By Vice-Admiral W. Usborne Moore. (London: Watts & Co., 1912.)

supposed to come from Galileo and Sir Isaac Newton. One of these affirms the existence of a planet in the solar system beyond the orbit of Neptune; the other denies it. Imagine the two greatest modern astronomers, untrammelled by earthly limitations and enriched with the experience of centuries, contradicting one another on so elementary a question of fact! Yet this is typical of the character of these messages from the other world. No hint of any new discovery, no glimmer of any addition to our hard - won human knowledge, has ever emanated from beyond the veil. If we were to believe in mediumistic messages, we should be forced to conclude that human originality is a myth, that almost every thought, every invention, every discovery that men have made has been communicated to them by the discarnate minds of those who have gone before. But such a thought is as baseless as it is revolting. Some of Admiral Moore's "controls" informed him that the discoveries of Mr. Edison were due to suggestions from disembodied spirits. This assertion calls to mind the photograph in the recently published "Life of Edison," which depicts him as he appeared after working five days and nights on end on the phonograph. After such herculean labour, after such intense and marvellous concentration upon his task, we are to be told that the man himself deserves no credit for his invention — that it has been given to him by suggestion from incorporeal minds!

Why, if such things are possible, do we never get any

intimation of impending disaster from these ubiquitous spirits? It happened while Admiral Moore's book was passing through the press that his little grandchild was burned alive in its cot, through the negligence of a nurse. A week or more afterwards the spirits turned up in the séance-room to assure the bereaved relative that the little one was happy and well cared for in the other world. But, needless to say, no hint had come to him before, warning him to prevent this distressing catastrophe. Such is the invariable course of things in these messages from beyond. They are, without exception, fatuous and useless. They consist of matter which not even a spiritist would think worth the cost of ink and paper if they were believed to come from living human minds; but because of the weird interest attaching to manifestations believed to be occult, they are trumpeted as revelations and made the basis for a vast mountain of inference which is totally devoid of scientific warrant.

Of course, the robust faith of the spiritist provides him with an answer to this criticism. The mind and body of the medium, he tells us, furnish only a very unsatisfactory and refractory instrument for these communications. The medium is only "a tele-graph-office"; and our experience of that marvellous agency, the Western Union Telegraph Company, warns us to expect something more than ordinary human fallibility in the operations of such a machinery. In the lecture on "The Immortality of the Soul" which Sir Oliver Lodge has reprinted in his book called "Man and the Universe," he says: "It must be admitted that in all cases, the manner and accidents or accessories of the messages are liable to be modified by the material instrument or organ through which the thought or idea is for our information reproduced." It must indeed be admitted! And on the same principle we must admit that messages may be *created* by the sub-conscious mind whose operations are correlative to the medium's brain and body.

It is perhaps unnecessary to point out the difference between such an after-life as spiritism and ordinary orthodox teaching affirm and the conception of eternity which their philosophy implies. No picture of the Christian heaven has ever been able to escape the infection of temporality and spatiality. Even Keble, the most orthodox of poets, is forced to declare that the common ideas of heaven are "poor fragments all of this low earth." Neither spiritualism nor popular theology has been able to grasp or willing to accept the implications of *eternity* as distinguished from protracted temporality. Milton, declaiming in his splendid rhetoric about "the dateless and irrevoluble circle of eternity," speaks in the same breath of *progression*. But progression is exactly what the concept of eternity excludes. Eternity stands opposed to time, as perfection to imperfection, without before and after, embracing in a timeless moment past, present and future. The "eternal glance" of which the German philosophers speak is a necessary implication of their thought, inconceivable as it may be to minds limited as ours are. To believe, then, in an after-life trammelled by time and space, is not to escape from materialism or to attain to the standpoint of eternity.

There is one lesson forced upon us by Sir Oliver Lodge's advocacy of the survival of man which it is very important for the world to learn. We see already around us signs of a revolt against the expert. The revolt is a healthy one. Its necessity is probably not the fault of the expert as such, but it does arise from the altogether excessive deference which the public has been accustomed to give to his authority. What we are learning now is that one must beware of the expert outside his province. Sir Oliver Lodge is undoubtedly one of the greatest of living physicists; and any utterance which he may make within the sphere of his special competence commands the respectful attention of the layman. But anybody who compares those parts of his Presidential Address in which he discusses physics, with the paragraphs in which he talks about human survival, can see that he has an enormously more rigorous standard of accuracy in his own sphere than in this other region, in which he is only an adventurous amateur. His belief in immortality is based on evidence that he would not look at in a physics laboratory; and, apart from the quality of the evidence, he draws from it conclusions far outrunning the infer-

ences that would be justified if the evidence were
sound. We must learn, then, that the very eminence
of a man in his own sphere is a reason for suspecting
his deliverances on things outside it. That very concentration of attention, through many years, which
enables him to speak with authority in one branch of
science, inevitably excludes such specialized preparation and continuous concentration in another field as
would entitle him to authority there. The expert,
then, in physics or biology, is no more to be trusted
than a well - equipped layman when he speaks on
problems of psychology.

It is worthy of note in this connection that the
specialists in mental science are seldom or never converted to Sir Oliver Lodge's belief. Men whose special
training and lifelong discipline have lain in the field
of psychology are not prepared, upon the evidence, to
believe in human survival. Such men as Professor
Leuba, Professor Morris Jastrow, and even William
James, fall far short of the dogmatism of Sir Oliver
Lodge, Sir William Crookes, the late W. T. Stead
and our other distinguished amateurs of the séance-
room. The inclusion of Professor James's name in this
category of the sceptical may come as a surprise to
those unacquainted with his final utterances on the
subject. Yet in his posthumous volume of "Memories
and Studies" he quite definitely declared that after
twenty years of psychical research he was still "on the
fence" as regards the question whether man survives

bodily death. Sir Oliver Lodge ought to be in the same position; and his presence in the camp of the convinced believers is evidence that, with him as with the rest of them, the wish is father to the thought.

Despite all this criticism, however, I would reiterate that my own position involves no denial either of survival or even of immortality. My standpoint is that of complete agnosticism. Immortality for me is no more proved than it is disproved. I protest against the investigation of this subtle and difficult question by persons like Admiral Moore, whose incompetence is grotesquely apparent, and who are animated by a motive which would vitiate all results, even if the students were relatively competent. The ideal way to handle the problem would be to entrust it to a fairly large commission, composed of men wholly devoid of predilection, and thoroughly trained in the finest and most exact methods of observation which modern psychology has elaborated. To them should be handed over the Eusapia Palladinos, the Mrs. Pipers and the rest of the wonderful people capable of functioning as vehicles for minds other than their own conscious ones. It should be the business of the commissioners to eliminate such evidence as contains signs of fraud or of unconscious dissimulation, and to sift the tenuous residue in the most searching manner, so that they could present to the public whatever fragments of indisputable inference might be extractible from the data. If such a commission were to work continuously and to report, let us say, at ten- or twenty-year intervals, it is possible that in a century we might obtain sufficient evidence to justify a definite affirmative opinion. Until such searching and competent investigation has been completed, we have no right to decide; or, if we do decide, we must admit that our position is due not to evidence but to *a priori* faith or unfaith.

The loss of belief in immortality can make no difference to the moral outlook of humanity. One's only interest in the subject from an ethical point of view is to show that morality is richer and purer when the thought of an after-life has been eliminated than when that thought is brought in as an incentive. The universe has no terrors for the man who has overcome the fear of death. But there is obviously something defective in the righteousness which needs the stimulus of the hope of immortality, or the spur of the fear of punishment after death. To buttress morality with such hopes and fears is to degrade it. We may confidently trust that if the vision of a life hereafter fades more and more from the minds of men there will be a more general readiness to do justice, to love mercy, and to walk humbly before the ideal which we worship, than has ever been induced by the machinery of unwarrantable hope and fear resorted to by religion in the past.

CHAPTER V

THERE could be no completer misunderstanding of the age in which we live than that opinion which regards it as indifferent to religion. To many of the traditional forms of religion and to the organizations which stand for these it is indeed indifferent; but this attitude is wholly distinct from apathy in regard to the fundamental problems of which our traditional theologies assume to offer the solution. Indeed, the very refusal of many men and women to accept orthodox answers to the soul's questions arises from a profounder intellectual honesty, a deeper sincerity — in other words, a more truly religious spirit — than has ever prevailed before.

If evidence be needed of the intense yearning, the inarticulate desire of the present age for a new canalization of the spirit of religion, it lies ready to hand in every public library. The output of books dealing with the questions of God and the soul, of conversion, of conduct and character here and of a life hereafter, is altogether unprecedented. We may quite safely follow in this case the economic principle which connects supply with demand. Books to-day are published for profit; and the presence in the market of innumerable works on religion is demonstrative evidence of the existence of a widespread public interest in the subject. Every new message has an enthusiastic hearing; and a hearing, moreover, which is not evidence of a mere Athenian curiosity, but one backed by substantial monetary support. The world is really on tiptoe of creative expectancy, awaiting and demanding a new religion which shall satisfy the old need for inward harmony and reconciliation with the order of things.

Another clue to the mind of an age, which we may safely trust, is furnished by its fiction. The themes which novelists choose are always those in which they have reason to expect a considerable measure of public interest, and even in their most incredible characters the lineaments of their times are inevitably reflected or refracted. Now if we compare the fiction of to-day with that of a hundred or even fifty years ago, we find that the religious *motif* has in contemporary novels a prominence altogether new. The clerics and the religious-minded laymen in our older fiction are beset by no theological difficulties and by no discomforting sense of a clash between the ethical standards of their faith and the established social order. Parson Thwackum in "Tom Jones" is typical of his era. "When I mention religion," he says, "I mean the Christian religion; and not only the Christian religion, but the Protestant religion; and not only the Protestant religion, but the Church of England." He is troubled by no misgiving as to the permanent power of the religion of the Church of England to satisfy all the needs of the human spirit, nor are there in his circle any auditors to embarrass him with perplexing questions. The case is the same in the great fiction of the nineteenth century. When Dickens introduces a clergyman, he is of the type of the Reverend Frank Milvey in "Our Mutual Friend," whose only serious problem in life is that of making a wholly inadequate salary meet the needs of a more than adequate family. For the rest, we find in Dickens incredible Stigginses and Chadbands, but never a minister of religion whose faith causes him any searchings of soul. Even George Eliot's parsons — the Amos Bartons, the Mr. Gilfils and Mr. Casaubons — have no credal perplexities. She never depicts a clergyman undergoing that painful process of detachment from the old moorings with which her own experience had made her familiar.

It is with Mrs. Humphry Ward's memorable story of "Robert Elsmere" that the figure of the heretical clergyman comes prominently into fiction; and Elsmere was only the leader of a long procession. The repeated presentation in fiction of this situation is testimony, if any were needed, to the increasing commonness of a tragic fact in life. A clergyman signs a formula or a set of articles, defining a faith which he in all honesty has accepted in his childhood, only to find, as his experience of life broadens and his studies of the past grow more profound, that it is literally impossible in the present day for a thoroughly educated man to accept the traditional creeds in the traditional sense. He is then confronted with the painful dilemma either of stifling his conscience to save his living or of sacrificing the prospects of wife and children on the altar of his own mental integrity.

Mr. Winston Churchill has faced this situation, and in his recent novel he presents what is apparently his own solution of the religious problem, as well as his conception of the practical course which a clergyman so placed should adopt. "The Inside of the Cup" is the profoundest presentation of its theme yet given to us in fiction. My reason for rating the book thus highly is twofold. First, Mr. Churchill's heretical clergyman becomes aware of the ethical gulf between the faith and the lives of his wealthy parishioners, as well as of the difficulties presented by the creeds; and secondly, the author makes his hero, after the new revelation has come to him, decide to stay within the Church instead of abandoning his position there.[1]

Of Mr. Churchill's powers of literary craftsmanship it is perhaps late in the day to speak. He has had the courage to revive the long novel. It is true that he has not yet attained to the dimensions of Dickens and Thackeray, but he does present us with canvases large enough to allow for detailed pictures of the minds of his characters. And, despite the length of his books, they do not fail to satisfy that difficult canon of literary

[1] On this second point, however, it is only fair to remember that Mr. Churchill was anticipated by Mrs. Humphry Ward in *The Case of Richard Meynell*.

criticism which was laid down by Mr. Samuel Weller. When Mr. Weller, Senior, criticizes the abrupt ending of his son's love-letter in the words, "That's rayther a sudden pull-up, Sammy," his son demurs on the ground that "She'll wish there was more of it, and that's the great art o' letter-writin'." It is certainly a tribute to Mr. Churchill's art that after five hundred closely printed pages he generally leaves his reader wishing there was more of it.

Another characteristic of this writer's work that fully justifies his wide popularity is his power of seizing some main trend of the nation's evolution and linking up with this the detailed development of the careers of his characters. He does not give, as did Dickens, pictures of quiet lives apparently quite unconnected with the evolution of the social group amidst which they live. Mr. Churchill's characters live in time, and therefore they grow and change; the creations of Dickens inhabit eternity, and neither wax nor wane. Mr. Churchill watches what main currents draw the years, and in the marshalling of his characters and incidents we are conscious of the great trend as well as of private and personal developments.

In "The Inside of the Cup" he seems less at his ease with his theme than in earlier novels—such, for example, as "Coniston" and "The Crisis." One feels more sense of strain and effort in the working-out of the plot. This is doubtless due to the nature of the subject-matter, and, though an artistic defect, it indicates the seriousness with which the novelist has faced his task. There is the same skill in characterization to which Mr. Churchill's readers are accustomed. The men, as usual, are highly individualized and differentiated; and the women, also as usual, are better than the men. The heroine is a worthy successor to Virginia Carvel and Cynthia Wetherell — a blend of them, with perhaps an infusion of Miss Letitia Penniman. Unfortunately, as the plot develops, the author becomes so interested in his hero and heroine, and in the spiritual interests that absorb them, that he forgets all about the other characters, so that the close of the book is a tangle of loose ends, and we do not learn what becomes of several people in whom we are interested. But perhaps this means that there is to be a sequel.

A very brief résumé of the chief points of the story will facilitate the reader's appreciation of my criticism. We are introduced to the members of the most fashionable Episcopal church in a great city of the Middle West, whose old rector, Dr. Gilman, has recently died. The younger people of the congregation are troubled by the disharmony between the religious teaching they have received and the scientific principles and historical beliefs imbibed in their university courses. They, however, have no hand in the appointment of Dr. Gilman's successor. The vestry, whose task it is to fill the vacant place, are a set of more or less sincerely orthodox men, who yet have no intention of permitting the Church as an ethical force to interfere with the conduct of their business lives. They are capitalists to a man, and almost all of them under the thumb of a master spirit, Eldon Parr, a multi-millionaire who has risen from nothing by means of financial genius and unscrupulousness. The vestry under the circumstances naturally want a "safe" man, "one who does not mistake Socialism for Christianity," and who can be relied upon to preach the same gospel that they have always listened to. As seems to be usual in modern business, they turn for help to their corporation lawyer, one Langmaid, who undertakes a journey to the New England town in which he was born, for the purpose of importing a suitable rector. He returns with the Reverend John Hodder, who has never yet said an unorthodox word and has given no evidence of possessing anything so stupendous and dangerous as a political or economic opinion. The vestry are delighted with Langmaid's discovery, and Hodder is universally liked by the congregation, although the younger members of it remain as dissatisfied as ever, feeling that there is some invisible barrier which prevents them from getting into contact with his mind.

A year or so in his new parish brings about a total change in the new incumbent's outlook. After a period of singular friendship with Eldon Parr, based largely on pity for the man's solitude and evident unhappiness, he begins to discover disquieting evidence of the way in which his chief vestryman's wealth and power have been built up. He hears whispers of a financial trans-

action over the street-car service, by which unprofit-
able lines, quietly purchased by Parr and his associates,
had been re-sold to themselves under another name
at a fabulous price, paid by the unsuspecting public
in return for worthless stock and share certificates.

Distressed by his inability to get the slum people
into his church, Hodder goes on quest in the slums,
where he speedily stumbles across reality and the
twentieth century. The first and finest person he meets
there, Mr. Horace Bentley, proves to be one whom
Parr had quietly but legally robbed of his fortune
twenty years before. Hodder makes Bentley's acquaintance when 'trying to minister to the wife and
sick child of one Garvin, a workingman who had in-
vested his life's savings of five thousand dollars in the
Consolidated Traction enterprise, on the strength of
his faith in Eldon Parr, only to lose every cent he had.
Broken in health by his loss, and unable to find em-
ployment, the poor fellow finally resorts to suicide.
Hodder also learns that one of his leading vestrymen,
Ferguson, proprietor of the city's greatest department
store, is paying to the girls in his employ wages which
impel many of them to a life of shame.

On the other hand, the rector's confidence in the
orthodox faith is severely shaken by the questions put
to him by some of the finest young people in his congregation. He also undergoes serious searching of soul
when asked by a Mrs. Constable, whom he highly
respects, to re - marry her divorced daughter. As a

High Churchman, holding the Catholic theory of the indissolubility of marriage, he feels compelled to decline the request; but the incident leaves a permanent mark upon him. Perplexed and bewildered at the abysses which seem suddenly to have opened beneath his feet, he decides to stay in the city for the summer instead of going East on a vacation, and gives up his time to study and thought, with the result that by the end of the summer he has arrived at a reconstruction of his creed and an insight into social problems, on the strength of which he feels compelled to remain in the Church, but to preach a gospel fundamentally different from that which he had formerly expounded.

If I may venture on a word of criticism, I would say that Mr. Hodder is, on the one side, incredibly innocent when he leaves his New England parish, and that on the other, his development when confronted with the new problems is almost inconceivably rapid. It is difficult to believe that a man so active-minded could have remained all his life so blind to the economic and social facts of contemporary society as he is represented as being. Nor is it altogether *vraisemblable* that a clergyman should arrive so rapidly at a comparatively mature reconstruction and reinterpretation of faith, such as that which Hodder attains in the course of one summer's reading. Nor, again, is the logic of his apparent inference from the corrupt lives of his vestrymen to the falsity of the creed they profess altogether convincing. Many a High Churchman is entirely clear-sighted as to the conditions under which wealth is to-day produced and distributed, and perfectly aware of the irreconcilable clash between the ethical code professed by millionaires in church on Sunday and that upon which they act on the other days of the week. Yet these High Churchmen do not conclude that the faith professed on Sunday must therefore be false. They maintain rather that it is the very truth of the doctrine which makes it serviceable as a cloak for hypocrisy. It is the very elevation of the ethical standard of Christianity which makes the unscrupulous exploiter of his fellows desire the moral prestige which comes from lip-service to it.

Nor can we be fully satisfied with the theoretical reconstruction of religion in which Mr. Hodder finds rest. His new doctrine is widely held among honest and sincere clergymen of the modern type; but it is not a solution satisfactory to those who have really penetrated to the heart of things. Its supernaturalistic theism is taken for granted, and, although Hodder repudiates the miraculous doctrines of the incarnation and resurrection of Christ, he yet inconsistently retains Christ as the central sun of his moral and spiritual system. The real trend of democratic religion in our time is leading us quite away from this placing of Christ at the centre of the spiritual universe. The change is analogous to that which took place in astronomy when men ceased to look upon the earth as the centre of the world and discovered that the sun is the pivot of the solar system. Just as the physical world is no longer geocentric, so the spiritual world can no longer be Christo-centric. Deep and grateful as our reverence for the Founder of Christianity may be, we can no longer assent to the claim that he is unique, unapproachable, and all-sufficient for the spiritual, ethical and intellectual needs of human society.

Yet Mr. Hodder's resting-place is far in advance of his starting-point. It is a great moral progress to abandon, as he does, the doctrines of the virgin birth and physical resurrection of Christ, not as impossibilities but as impertinences. These theories (the former of which was not in the Gospels as they were first written, and the latter of which has clearly grown out of subjective visions like that of St. Paul) are visibly the invention of pedantic and unspiritual minds, who felt that the greatness and purity of the character of Christ needed to be accounted for miraculously. We are to-day advancing to the point where we see goodness to be as much a part of man's nature as sin. Our sense of the inherent dignity of humanity is teaching us that it is not the greatness of the great and the purity of the pure which need to be explained, but the littleness and baseness of the mass of men. It is these qualities which we feel to be inconsistent with humanity. The great, pure, clear-eyed personality embodies what we expect of mankind. He is the norm, the standard; and it is declensions from this standard which we feel called upon to explain. Thus the chief case against the miraculous is now seen to be its moral irrelevance, — its implication that goodness and greatness in human character are unnatural, and only to be accounted for by irruptions of a higher order into the human sphere.

Probably the question most provocative of discussion in connection with Mr. Churchill's novel will be the one raised by Hodder's conduct in remaining in the Church after he has abandoned the traditional interpretation of the creeds and articles of religion which he had accepted. As this is the most important issue which the book raises, we may be pardoned for dealing with it at some length.

The answer to the question whether an heretical clergyman has a moral right to remain in his Church (until such time as his plain speaking leads to his expulsion) must depend upon one's view of the nature and sociological function of the Church. That nature and function cannot be discovered by reading the Church's official account of itself. It would doubtless explain (as it does in the Athanasian Creed) that it exists to maintain the integrity of the theological faith of its members, to preserve undiluted the doctrine entrusted to its charge, and thus to secure the salvation of souls in a life after death. Its explanation would carry with it the implication that any man who does not hold strictly every article of its creed has neither part nor lot in its communion; and consequently it would expect the Hodders and Robert Elsmeres to resign their livings the moment they can no longer conscientiously proclaim the traditional theories.

We shall learn, however, to take a truer view of the nature and function of the Church if we compare it with the civil State. The civil State at any given moment is committed to the upholding of a certain constitution and certain laws. Yet nobody expects a man who desires changes in those laws or that constitution to expatriate himself from the State and to remain apart from it until the alterations he desires have been effected. On the contrary, we all recognize that there is no absolute finality about written laws and constitutions; and that it is often precisely the most patriotic citizen who desires to bring about changes in them. We see, therefore, that there is no conflict between the retention of citizenship and the desire for innovation in the State.

Now those who frankly take, as I do, the view that the Church is every whit as much a human institution as the civil State, can find no difficulty in reconciling the retention of church membership with desire for change in ecclesiastical creeds and formulas. We maintain that it was not the creeds that produced the Church, but the Church that produced the creeds. The Church, therefore, is prior to its own formulations. They were made for it, not it for them; therefore the Church is lord also of its creeds. We maintain that the function of the Church in the world is to act as the standard-bearer of human ideals, to insist upon the distinction between the life of the senses and the life of the spirit, to release the "angel heart of man" from the grip of ape and tiger, and to make channels for the streams of human love and service, so that the finer energies of the spirit may be released from the trammels of the baser nature, both of the individual and of society, and poured forth in beneficent service to all.

It must necessarily follow from such a conception that the Church not only may, but does, carry within itself the forces and machinery by which to effect its own evolutionary transformation. A Church fettered absolutely to the past, incapable of revising its creeds and formularies, would be as unnatural an institution as a civil State which could not modify or repeal any of its old laws or enact any new ones. Such bondage to the letter and to the dead hand of the past is totally at variance with the post-Darwinian conception of life as a process of growth and change. A Church which was really in the position in which Catholics suppose their Church to stand would be not merely an anachronism but a downright impossibility. The eternal self-identity which the Catholic communion boasts must consist, if it be a fact, not in the formulated theology of creed and catechism, but in an immutable bent of will and direction of purpose, which, because it animated the old creeds, can for that very reason supersede them and reinterpret itself in fresh formulations.

It is, therefore, perfectly possible and consistent for a man to remain in a Church whose creed he desires to change, just as it is possible for a man to remain a loyal citizen of a State whose laws and constitution he sees to need revision. For my own part, then, I entirely approve of the conduct of Mr. Churchill's hero in claiming the right to utter from the pulpit his new social vision and his new insight into the history, development and purpose of the Church.

The popular feeling on this matter is, to be sure, against Mr. Hodder, and in favour of the demands of the old-fashioned believers within the Church. This popular feeling is expressed in the colloquial phrase that a man ought not to stay "where he doesn't belong." But suppose we agree to this statement; the question will still remain to be decided, Where does such a man "belong"? If it be true that the Church stands ideally for moral integrity, for truth and truthfulness, for conformity between thought and speech, and for the supremacy of the ethical ideal in every region of conduct, how can it be that a man who is more than ordinarily sincere, who is too honest to pretend to believe what he does not believe, who feels like a wound the stain of uttering with his mouth a belief that his conscience denies, must for that very reason abandon his post in the spiritual army? Do we not feel the absurdity of a course of action on the part of such a man which implies that he has neither part nor lot in the one organization which stands for ideals, and that his true place is in the world of secular and material interests — that world which is dominated by the lust for money and the goods which money can purchase?

Those who, for the sake of the ideal interests of nations, desire the well-being of the Church, and yet feel that the innovating thinker ought to abandon it, would do well to reflect on the position which would have ensued if Mr. Hodder had resigned his charge at St. John's. It is significant that it is precisely the enemies of justice and righteousness who wish him to do this. The morally blind financiers, the uneasy hypocrites who own houses which are let for purposes of vice, and who are consciously pocketing rents enhanced by this consideration; the employers of sweated labour who only want to maintain the Church as a bulwark against that social indignation which would imperil the possession of their ill-gotten gains — these it is who demand that the brave heretic should abandon his post, and who even offer him a concealed bribe, in the shape of a possible missionary bishopric, if he will hold his tongue and step aside. In other words, the inevitable result which follows when men of new vision and exalted spirit resign from the Church is that the Church is left tenfold more in the grip of corruption than before. The forces of darkness and retrogression are strengthened and entrenched, and the man who steps aside from the historical organization of moral idealism inevitably dooms himself to comparative obscurity and ineffectuality.

If proof of a statement so obvious be needed, I would cite the case of the great ethical movement of our own day within the Roman Catholic Church. The one religious development of modern times which has secured universal attention is that of the school of the Abbé Loisy and the late Father Tyrrell. These are men full of the spirit which places the things of the moral world above the things of the sense - world. These, on the spiritual side, are worthy successors to Thomas à Kempis, to Francis of Assisi and to Francis of Sales; but they are also permeated with the modern spirit of intellectual integrity, with the love of exact accuracy which science engenders, and with a determination to reformulate, at whatever cost, their theory of the spiritual life in harmony with that life itself as they experience it. They insist on their right to remain members of the Catholic Church and to utter from within its borders the new revelation which has come to men in modern days. By leaving the Church they would have played into the hands of their enemies. They would have been quietly ignored, as many another equally fine spirit has been. But by remaining within the Church they compelled the worldly-minded coterie of the Vatican to take notice of them, and to meet their arguments — as best it could. The result was that by the papal Encyclical against Modernism and by Cardinal Mercier's egregious Lenten Pastoral against Father Tyrrell, the Vatican and its instruments made themselves intellectually and morally the laughing-stock of Europe. Inadvertently they gave to Modernism a publicity and a prestige which it could not otherwise have secured, and which are sufficiently great to make permanent and imperishable the work of George Tyrrell and his coadjutors.

The result of the alternative policy can be shown to have been unqualifiedly disastrous to mankind. When the Reformation broke out, the finest spirits desired to reform the Church from within, so as to avoid the necessity of schism. Such men as Erasmus and Colet and Sir Thomas More saw as clearly as did Luther the necessity for reformation. No reader of Erasmus's "Commentaries on the New Testament" can doubt that he stood as emphatically for ethical Christianity, and was as strong in his repudiation of the mountain-heaps of mediæval dogmatism, as any Modernist to-day. To More's liberality of thought, and to his profound and far-sighted conviction of the possibility of religious union without credal uniformity, the " Utopia " is a perennial witness. These men and their fellow-Humanists desired a radical purgation of the Church, both moral and intellectual. The greatest disaster of the modern world was the failure of this policy. The successors of Luther acquiesced in their expulsion from the Church. They accepted their position as outsiders, thereby implicitly admitting that they had no right within the Catholic fold, — and also that the obscurantists, the friends of spiritual tyranny and moral obliquity, were entitled to monopolize the wealth, the prestige and the artistic and cultural traditions of the Church.

From then till now, the individualistic insanity of separatism has continued, until we have become blind to the true function of religion and of the Church in the life of nations. We no longer perceive that religion is virile and beneficent only when it is felt to be the soul of national and international life. We overlook the fact that every nation, in so far as it has ideals for itself and for mankind, is a Church, to which every one of its citizens belongs, both in actual fact and by moral right, and whether he knows it or not. We think of religion as a private, personal relation between a man and some supernatural source of character and power; and the natural outcome of the practices begotten of such an illusion is that religion is perverted and deformed into anti-social absurdities like Christian Science and Mormonism, and every nation of the modern world is spiritually divided against itself.

Whoever has studied the history and the surviving monuments of mediæval Europe can see at a glance what was the sociological function of the Catholic Church. That Church may give what account of itself it chooses; but the student of history, psychology and sociology knows that it did in fact serve as the organ-

izer and unifier of the life of mediæval nations. The
halls of the City Companies in London, where the
merchant guilds formerly met, with their patron saints
and their religious observances connecting commerce
with the common ideals, testify to the union between
mediæval industry and the larger spiritual life within
which it was integrated. The Church was undeniably
the patron of art, of painting, of music, of sculpture, of
architecture, and even of the drama. If the Catholic
Church was, as Matthew Arnold said, "The prophetic
soul of the world dreaming on things to come," it was a
soul which more and more was individuating itself into
nationalities and solidary group-consciousnesses; and
the utter collapse of this unifier of the life of men,
which ensued through the wrong policy that prevailed
in the Reformation, was the direct cause of the spiritual chaos which prevails in the world to-day.

Whereas of old the various interests of life were
articulated into an interdependent system, the lower
subordinated to the higher, and the whole of life ori-
ented towards spiritual goals, there is now scarcely any
bond of union within or between nations except that
of economic interest. The cash nexus, which is the
confession that we are united only in our sordid and
material ambitions — this is the one universal bond of
modern humanity. If the policy of Erasmus and More
and Colet had been followed out in the past four hundred years, we should have had a world no longer at
sixes and sevens on its spiritual side and united only in

its material interests, but a world in which national and international politics, industry, art, education and science would have been blent into an overarching unity of common ideal purpose. We should have had a Church at once truly national and truly catholic. We should have had humanity fulfilling itself in many ways, in virtue of a conscious unity of ideal purpose and goal. If it be not too late for the world to attain such unity, still the unification can only be effected through a reinterpretation of religion and a reconstruction of the Church. And this can most speedily be rendered possible by an absolute refusal on the part of those whose profession identifies them with the ideal, to abandon that profession when their vision broadens and their knowledge deepens.

I am not oblivious to the difficult moral problem which confronts the heretical clergyman in regard to the use of the traditional creeds. Those creeds are embodied in the liturgy of the Episcopal Church, and Mr. Churchill's hero feels bound to repeat them until constitutional authority releases him from the obligation. But it is a blind illiteracy which holds that the creeds of Christendom are so univocal and definitive in their meaning that there can be no variety in the interpretation placed upon them. There is, it is true, no more difficult and embarrassing task than that of the man who goes about to interpret an ancient document in a sense which it has been commonly assumed to exclude. The keener his insight, the subtler his

intelligence, and the profounder his honesty, the more
is he liable to misunderstanding and denunciation.
Such, for example, was the fate of John Henry Newman, when, in an effort to reconcile his changed beliefs
with his position in the English Church, he sought
to place a Catholic construction on the Thirty-nine
Articles. The epithet of hypocrite was promptly
hurled at him. Obviously, no real hypocrite would
have subjected himself to the exhausting labour and
the danger of misunderstanding which Newman faced.
It was, indeed, only the exceptional sincerity of the
man which set him upon his task. Like all acute thinkers, he could see various intermediate shades of grey
where the vulgar herd could detect only dead blacks
and whites. The final resignation of Newman was an
injury to the Church of England from which it has
scarcely yet recovered. Its result was to cramp the
mental freedom of all who remained within her borders
— not only the High Church, but also the Broad
Church and the Evangelical parties.

To return for a moment to our analogy between
Church and State: is it not obvious that for a man to
abandon the Church because of corruption within it,
or because he finds its dogmas incredible, is exactly
akin in its results to what happens when men abandon
political parties because of corruption within them?
The tragedy of American life to-day, as everybody
admits, is the reluctance of good men to enter political
life. They feel that they cannot touch its pitch without

being defiled; and the result is that those who have
no antipathy to the pitch are left, in many cities and
States, with almost a monopoly. The only cure for
corruption in municipal, State and national politics
consists in the invasion of political party life by men
who have no price, and whose single purpose is the
patriotic desire to promote the common good. By
standing aloof they only encourage and entrench the
shameless exploiters of the nation's life.

Now, Edmund Burke's famous dictum that "when
bad men combine, the good must unite," applies in
religious life as well as in political. And they must
unite in opposition not only to conscious badness, but
also to moral blindness, and to the erroneous view
which mistakes the dogmas of religion for the life
of religion. They must persistently refuse to abandon
their standing - ground because of apparent inconsistency between their intellectual positions and the
traditional ones of the Church.

A rule for the guidance of clergymen in Mr. Hodder's
position might well be formulated in the blunt phrase,
"Stay in and speak out. Don't leave until you are
kicked out." Many men of refined and sensitive spirit
resign their pulpits because they cannot face the worry
of perpetual squabbling, and also because they think
it undignified to be expelled. But it is perfectly dignified to face expulsion when the question at issue is no
mere personal one, but one that involves the fate of a
great historic institution, which still stands nominally,

as it always should have stood in fact, for the supremacy of the higher life of man.

The present conditions of tenure of office for clergymen place a direct premium upon insincerity and hypocrisy. The devil himself could have invented nothing more ingeniously maleficent than the system which makes a man's bread and butter depend upon his continuous profession of a definitely formulated belief, whether he holds it or not. One of the many stories told of Benjamin Jowett at Oxford is that, when his duties necessitated his reciting the creed in chapel, he would insert *sotto voce* the words "used to," so that his creed ran, "I *used to* believe in God the Father," and so forth. The delightful humour of the legend cannot conceal the danger of demoralization incurred by clergy whose opinions are as heretical as Jowett's. One cannot help suspecting (and the suspicion is justified by many actual experiences which one is not at liberty to relate) that if a philanthropic fund made it possible for clergymen, who got into trouble with their denominational authorities through sincere speech, to maintain their families after expulsion, there would be such an outburst of what is called heresy in all orthodox bodies as to compel a radical transformation of the theories of Christianity.

The day of the heresy-hunt is not yet over, and even in a community so modern as Chicago there have been cases where sincere speech has brought down upon men's heads the thunderbolts of the *odium theologicum*.

The one thing that I regret upon reading the life of Professor Swing, the great Presbyterian preacher of Chicago, is that after the heresy-hunt against him had failed he resigned from the Presbyterian body, because he could not bear to be involved in perpetual bickerings and controversy. American Presbyterianism would to-day be broader, humaner and nobler, if Swing had insisted on his right to freedom of thought and speech within that body. On the other hand, it is delightful to know that when an attempt was made some years ago to expel Professor George Burman Foster from the Baptist denomination, he insisted, with irresistible logic and masterly scholarship, that he was as good a Baptist as any of his opponents, and had a perfect moral right to remain within the same fold with them. As a result of his success in carrying this point, the Baptist Church to-day is a finer thing, and truer to its own original inspiration, than it would have been if the heresy-hunters had been suffered to prevail.

The foregoing rule for modern-minded clergymen is applicable, *mutatis mutandis*, to the case of laymen. Let them, from within whatever body they may belong to, insist that the true function of the Church is not the maintenance of a formal creed but the purification of the common life of man. If they be Christians, let them insist that Christianity is primarily an ethical discipline, the standard of which is to be found in the Sermon on the Mount, the Parables and the social vision of the New Testament. Let them proclaim the obvious fact that the original test of membership in Christ's kingdom was not the acceptance of a creed but the will to serve one's neighbours. Or if they be Jews, let them point out — what every scholar knows to be the truth — that Judaism was originally the national idealism of the Hebrew people, with its interest neither in metaphysical theism nor in a life after death, but in politics, economics, civic law and domestic life. Let them maintain that the very spirit in the Jewish leaders which led them to change repeatedly their heaven-sent decalogue and to revise their religious law-codes from time to time to meet their exigencies, must to-day dictate a fundamental transformation of Jewish doctrine and discipline to meet the new conditions of the new age.

The clue to the spiritual unification of mankind is given us in an aphorism of W. K. Clifford's. "Only in a world of sincere men," he said, "is unity possible; but there, in the long run, it is as good as certain."

My argument leads inevitably to the personal question, "But why, if such be your view of the duties of people within the Church, are you the spokesman of an outside organization? Why are you the minister of an Ethical Society?" I answer that the social conception of religion, as moral idealism concreting itself in ethical nationalism, carries with it a discrimination between a sect and a party, which makes such a position entirely logical and clear. I have not space here to analyze this distinction, but in the works of Dr. Stanton Coit, who learned it not only through his studies of Biblical Judaism, but also from the profound teachings of Sir John Seeley, it is elaborated in detail.[1] Those in the Ethical Movement who hold this view conceive of their fellowship as a party within the national religious life, just as, for example, the Progressive Party is a factor in the political life of this nation. And as a political party does not isolate itself, but seeks to grapple with its opponents, for the very purpose of arriving at ultimate unity of national conviction and polity, so we conceive of all the denominations of religion as co-operative groups within the national spiritual life. Among these the Ethical Society has its natural place as the advanced wing, the pioneer party, in which tendencies visibly at work in all the other churches have come into clear consciousness. We are the enemies not of other denominations as such, but of the spirit and policy of sectarianism which still animate so many of them. We are the enemies of that conception of religion which rests satisfied with denominational self-dependence and isolation. We stand opposed to this spirit precisely because we believe in religion as necessary to humanity, and we know that only by the breaking down of credal barriers, only by the free intercourse of mind with mind and Church with Church (even though that intercourse at first involve antagon-

[1] See especially *The Soul of America*, by Stanton Coit. (New York: The Macmillan Company, 1914.)

ism and controversy), can ultimate unity be attained. We are not innovators in spirit and purpose. Rather for the sake of the eternal spirit and the abiding purpose of religion do we desire innovation, in order that the nobler energies of the human mind may be liberated and taught to co-operate. And we believe that the most effective declaration of their new attitude which modern-minded laymen in all denominations can make is to join the Ethical party without renouncing their other religious affiliations.

The modern attitude of the world toward religion is only partially expressed in Mr. Churchill's story by Eleanor Goodrich. Her mother, unable to meet the arguments of the young people, declares that an old woman must not be expected to change. Eleanor replies, "We don't want you to change. It's ourselves we wish to change. We wish for a religious faith like yours, only the same teaching which gave it to you is powerless for us." The Ethical Movement and the other advanced wings of Christianity and Judaism have been inspired, if I mistake not, by a like sentiment in relation to the more conservative churches. Only, instead of saying that we *wish* for a religious faith like theirs, we go further and proudly claim that we have such a faith. We are at one with the Hebrew prophets and with the founder and first apostles of Christianity *in bent of will and purpose;* but with our modern knowledge, and in view of the complexity of modern economic and social conditions, we say

frankly that the theoretical counterpart of this volitional attitude which satisfied the mind of fifteen hundred years ago is valueless for us. We hold that the
creeds were nothing but the best interpretation possible in their day to account to the intellect for the
bent of will and spirit of self-sacrifice with which it
was concretely associated in life. We maintain, further, that as experience widens every such theoretical
formulation necessarily becomes obsolete. Every age
ought to write its own creeds; but no future age will
fall into the grievous error of ascribing finality to its
formulations. The essence of religion, the eternal element in it, is the life and not the dogma, the bent of
will, the purpose of securing inward peace and social
salvation for mankind. Let this be expressed from
time to time in accordance with the fullest philosophic
and scientific knowledge; but let not the formula
become a fetter and a stumblingblock to the spirit
which engenders it.

CHAPTER VI

ELLEN KEY AND THE "NEW MORALITY" OF FREE LOVE [1]

It is difficult in these days for a man to give utterance to a platitude without incurring the suspicion that he is indulging in paradox. We have become so accustomed to subordinating our own judgment to the authority of a sophisticated literary minority, who confound the exceptional with the general, that even the restatement of an obvious fact sounds startling and incredible. Nevertheless, the rule remains the rule, and is more worthy of attention than any or all exceptions to it which may be cited; and so, at the risk of seeming paradoxical, one must turn first to it.

The startling platitude, then, which I would begin by formulating is simply this: that of all human institutions the most widely and permanently successful is that of lifelong monogamous marriage. A basis of experience incomparably great and long justifies the assertion that this method of providing for the physical and psychic needs of individuals, and for the continuance of the human species, is the one best adapted to these ends. If it were not so, no amount of coercion by

[1] *Love and Marriage*, translated from a Swedish work entitled *Lifslinjer*, by Ellen Key. The translation by Arthur G. Chater. With an Introduction by Havelock Ellis. (New York: Putnam, 1912.)

authority, whether ecclesiastical or civil, could have induced mankind permanently to endure it. Moreover, there is in modern communities very little left of this authoritative buttressing of monogamy. The chains have been broken, the whip wrested from the driver's hands; yet the slaves oddly persist for the most part in treading freely the accustomed path.

We hear much, to be sure, of the multiplication of divorces in countries like America, where legalized divorce is very easily obtainable. What we do not hear much of is the still more important fact that the number of divorces, huge and menacing as it is, remains insignificant as compared with the number of marriages *not* dissolved. The highest estimate I have seen of the total of divorces in this country places it at one in twelve of the total of marriages. Nor does this mean that of every twelve *couples* who marry one is sundered by divorce. The statistics are swelled by that naturally increasing number of men and women who, having once snapped an old bond and accepted a new, proceed to make a habit of getting themselves divorced. I recently read, for instance, in the newspaper the story of a gentleman who, having been married and divorced, formed a legal union with a second lady; tiring of this in a year or two, he was again divorced and reunited himself with his wife — I beg pardon, with his *first* wife; and the newspaper announced in hiccoughing head-lines the fact that he had gone off on a second honeymoon with the mother of his children." The reporter did not seem to think that the circumstances offered any occasion for moral censure. One does not look, indeed, to the ordinary newspaper for ethical sanity, any more than for general accuracy and competence in the presentation of fact; but the abstention from moral judgment in such a case as this was merely typical of the general trend of public opinion in the United States to-day. The tone of American *Sittlichkeit* with reference to divorce grows ever laxer. Beginning with tolerance of those whose unions were terminated for good cause, it has grown more and more willing to accept the divorced person, irrespective of the cause of his or her renunciation of the marriage vow. Yet, even with this added incentive to marital laxity, the fact remains that permanent monogamous union is deliberately preferred in eleven cases out of twelve.

We must pause to insist upon the significance of this fact. British critics of marriage, such as Mr. Bernard Shaw, affirm that the very small number of divorces in England is wholly due to the disastrously barbarous condition of the English divorce law. There is, of course, some truth in their assertion; but it is much less true than they imagine. A closer examination of the facts would disclose a truth which I here mention merely in passing, but to which I must return later: that the bond which unites man and wife is not merely the outward coercion of the law. The law only registers and reinforces an accomplished fact. It does not unite people; they unite themselves, and it ratifies and sanctions their union. The marriage "contract" is not so much between the man and the woman as between the two of the one part and the community of the other part. The strength of the marriage tie is accordingly natural and inherent, as well as artificial and adherent. The facts of American experience prove my point. Here is a vast and heterogeneous population in whom the sense of law and authority is very decidedly weaker than in Europe, and for whom divorce in many States is made dangerously easy. The restraining influence of religion upon this population is certainly no stronger, and almost certainly a great deal weaker, than it is in England. Yet with every opportunity for laxity, with law and public opinion standing ready to further their inclinations in that direction, this population, in the proportion of eleven to one, voluntarily prefers the lifelong monogamous marriage bond.

This is the colossal fact which we must bear carefully in mind when reading such outpourings as those of Mr. Shaw in the preface to "Getting Married," and of Miss Ellen Key in her book on "Love and Marriage." We must be careful to remember it, because these writers never mention it. Yet the fact is one which makes us detect a note of unconscious absurdity in the indictments they draw up against lifelong monogamy. If what they say were true, this irredeemably bad institution must long since have destroyed humanity. Mr. Shaw declares that the corner-

stone of the system which produces all our social disasters is "the family and the institution of marriage
as we have it [*sic*] to-day in England." [1] In similar fashion, Miss Ellen Key pictures marriage as an
incredibly savage and morally unendurable institution: —

> Whatever abuses free divorce may involve, they can-
> not often be worse than those which marriage has pro-
> duced and still produces — marriage, which is degraded
> to the coarsest sexual habits, the most shameless traffic,
> the most agonising soul - murders, the most inhuman
> cruelties, and the grossest infringements of liberty that
> any department of modern life can show. [2]

Whereupon one can only express a mild wonder that
the revolted conscience of mankind has not long since
risen and annihilated the abominable thing! But,
again, we must keep our balance — we must remember
the eleven couples out of twelve, who are as free to
dissolve their bonds as the one couple in twelve that
does so. How comes it that no glimmer of the ineffable
spiritual refinement of Mr. Shaw and Miss Key has
broken through the darkness of their souls?

The truth is that this modern attack on marriage,
in its one-sidedness, and its failure either to remember
the exceptionalness of the exceptional or to grasp the
good points of what it attacks, is almost grotesque. It
reminds one irresistibly of a ludicrous incident which

[1] *The Doctor's Dilemma*, etc., p. 120 (Preface to *Getting Married*).
(London: Constable, 1911.)
[2] *Love and Marriage*, p. 290.

happened a few years ago in England. One of the
cheap newspapers, — cheap in every sense of the word,
— wishing to advertise itself, started a campaign of
denunciation against the ordinary white bread of commerce. It declared that this bread contained none
of the nutritive properties of the grain, and therefore
that to eat it was merely to injure one's digestive system without receiving any benefit. For this reason, it
recommended to its readers a new kind, called "Standard Bread." The public was appalled, and began to
rush eagerly to the shops of those bakers whose signs
announced that they sold the new style of bread. The
bubble was pricked, however, when some man who
had not entirely lost his sense of humour arose and
asked, "What is the use of telling us that there is no
food value but only poison and disaster in a thing
upon which we have all been living healthily all our
lives?" To the credit of the English public be it said
that this self-evident fact at once convinced them of
the absurdity of their alarm. "Standard Bread" was
promptly forgotten, and the newspaper proceeded to
manufacture fresh methods of self-advertisement.

Which things are an allegory; and after reading Mr.
Shaw, Miss Key and a number of other wearisomely
old-fashioned [1] modern thinkers, one can only ask them
to resuscitate their comatose sense of humour. What
is the use of their telling us that marriage is anti-social,

[1] This adjective is used advisedly. The writers in question have
not an idea among them of later date than the fourth century B.C.
— as every reader of Plato's *Republic* knows.

anti-human, degrading and soul-murdering, and all the rest of it, when the nations of the world that are most advanced, both spiritually and economically, have been healthily living by it all their lives?

Miss Key, of course, is not backward in advocating what she thinks the right alternative to the system she condemns. Every healthy woman is to be recognized by law as having a right to motherhood, whether marriage be for her possible or desirable or not. She is to be safeguarded and respected by public opinion as well as by law, and pecuniary provision, when necessary, is to be made for her and for the children born under such conditions. The permanence, or otherwise, of her relations with the father (or fathers) of her children is to be nobody's business but her own, and none may dare to stigmatize either her male accessories or the offspring. Divorce is to be absolutely free and unconditional — that is, it is to be granted upon the request of both parties, *or of one*, provided such request be persisted in for a definite period. This involves the position that, however unwilling either the man or the woman may be to accept the sunderance, it is nevertheless to be effected. If a man tires of his wife, he notifies some legal official of the circumstance. A year later he reaffirms his decision, and automatically thereupon, without any question as to his reasons or his future intentions, the divorce is conceded. The fact that his wife, the mother of his children, may be absolutely innocent and violently opposed to the proceeding is not to count at all; nor are the children to be consulted.

It is obvious that, with divorce on such terms, with no questions asked, and with the right to extra-marital motherhood sanctioned by law to every woman (and, by necessary implication, the right to extra-marital fatherhood granted and guaranteed to every man), marriage would, so far as the law is concerned, be virtually abolished. The great principle of individualistic anarchism, that the relations of the sexes are the mere private affair of the persons immediately concerned, would be established. Public opinion might indeed continue upon eugenic grounds to uphold certain standards of chastity and continence; it might continue to maintain that the general and permanent well-being of the race must be the paramount consideration of every man and woman; but it could neither itself condemn nor ask the law to prohibit any making or breaking of unions between men and women.

It is only just that, before proceeding to criticism of such proposals, one should pay a tribute of respect to the purity and nobility of purpose which animate some, at least, of their advocates. In this category I wish quite unequivocally to place both Mr. Shaw and Miss Key. It would be wholly unfair to accuse or suspect either of them of anti-social intent. As my present concern is mainly with Miss Key, I wish to testify that the study of her works produces a strong conviction of her purity and sincerity in thought and purpose. She has also rendered an important service in two respects. First, she has, with admirable courage, laid bare a side of woman's nature which has generally been concealed from men, and to which men have consequently failed to do justice. She deserves credit for a perfect candour in this matter, without which its adequate discussion would be impossible, and also for a fine and discriminating artistic skill in the presentation of the facts, without which candour itself might be useless and would certainly be repellent. The second service for which I wish to thank her, relates to a matter in which she is at variance with Mr. Shaw and certain other critics of marriage and family life. She sees clearly that the family is the true social unit — "true" in the sense that it is necessitated by the physical and psychic nature and needs of the children. The child has a right to a father as well as to a mother, and its due "nurture and admonition" demands the co-operation of the two parents. How this doctrine can be made to consist with Miss Key's other proposals is a matter which we must leave to her to settle. What sort of homes those will be in which Johnny calls Mr. Jones his father to-day, and Mr. Brown next week, it is not at once easy to understand. There, however, is the situation; and I wish to acknowledge the soundness of Miss Key's plea for the home, while confessing my inability to understand how she reconciles it with her other proposals.

But, while admitting her nobility and purity of purpose, I find evidences in her work of two serious defects, which vitiate her practical proposals for remedying the evils associated with our present law and custom. She seems, in the first place, to suffer from a certain blindness in the discrimination of moral distinctions: that is, she frequently makes suggestions which imply that the moral quality of certain lines of action can be changed by changing their name, and that things immoral in themselves can be made right by being sanctioned by law. The second defect, correlative to this, is an inability to foresee the social consequences which would necessarily ensue if public sanction were given to her proposals. These are the chief shortcomings of her work. Her obliviousness to the evils which her doctrine would let loose upon society is in a certain sense honourable to her. She reasons too freely from her own æsthetic and ethical standards to those of humanity at large. Living herself on a plane of exaltation and serenity "above the smoke and stir of this dim spot which men call earth," she fails to realize the formidable strength of the baser nature in ordinary men and women, and, for that reason, does not see what floods of evil would be liberated by the removal of the locks and dams of law and social sentiment which at present restrain them. I shall subsequently set forth the evidence upon which these two assertions are based.

Probably the simplest and most convenient way of

introducing one's criticism will be to state one's own conviction as to the wise and right method of providing for the needs of individuals and of human society, in this supremely important matter. My own ideal, therefore, is that marriage should be a union of one man and one woman for so long as they both shall live. So old-fashioned a doctrine will not commend itself to those seekers after new truth who imagine that all old truth must be discarded when new is discovered. I may, however, succeed to some extent in placating them by the assertion that I hold this view in no sense upon the authority of any Church or of any theological creed. I do not believe in indissoluble monogamy because Christ commanded it. I am by no means certain that he did so. My belief in it reposes upon grounds of agelong and widespread human experience, and would remain unshaken, even if it could be shown that Christ had authorized polygamy, or if the Catholic Church were suddenly converted to Mormonism. My belief is a free conviction, resulting from long thought and from such study of historical and anthropological evidence as I have been able to make. I entirely agree with Miss Key that monogamy was made for man, and not man for monogamy. I hold, further, that monogamy was made by man, and has never at any time been commanded or ratified by any supernatural or superhuman agency. I am willing, also, to draw from these principles their logical conclusion — that if any other system than that of lifelong monogamy could be shown to meet better than it the physical, psychic and ethical needs of men and women, and to promote better than it the health, sanity and virility of the human race throughout all time, then monogamy would have to be abandoned, and that other system introduced. But what impresses a student of the world's experience in this matter is this simple fact: that all the alternative systems advocated by our modern theorists, instead of being, as they suppose, new and untried, are in fact old and discredited. Every possible alternative to lifelong monogamy is being or has been practised, and monogamy has won its pre-eminence by a protracted struggle for existence in which it gained the victory over all its rivals. This is the conclusion which emerges from the study of such a masterly work as Professor Westermarck's "History of Human Marriage."

There is one important fact, of which we in Christendom are almost entirely oblivious. It is this: that in times and places where polygamy and polyandry are sanctioned by law, opinion and religion, monogamy is, nevertheless, widely practised, and tends to predominate exactly in the proportion in which the community progresses towards civilization.[1] We commonly as-

[1] "Even in Africa, the chief centre of polygynous habits, polygyny is an exception.

"It is so among all Mohammedan peoples, in Asia and Europe as well as in Africa. 'In India,' says Syed Amir Ali, 'more than ninety-five per cent. of Mohammedans are at the present moment, either by conviction or necessity, monogamists.'" — Westermarck, *op. cit.*, p. 439.

sume, by an unconscious fallacy, that in a country
where polygamy is allowed, everybody practises it.
Apart from the fact that Nature makes this impossible,
through her obstinate persistence in producing men
and women in approximately equal numbers, it would
be quite as reasonable to assume that in countries
where divorce is legalized, everybody gets divorced.
The widespread practice of polygamy or polyandry,
however, is so generally discovered to be a correlative
of degraded barbarism as to justify the assumption
that where we find monogamy increasing and tending
to dominate (whether it be ordained by law and custom or not), civilization is advancing and social soundness and virility are being augmented. Such a fact
constitutes at least a strong presumption in favour
of the claim of monogamy to an even greater pre-
dominance than it has hitherto enjoyed.

I have spoken of the indissoluble lifelong bond as
being the *ideal* of the relation of the sexes. It is Miss
Key's ideal also. She imagines, however, that this
relation cannot exist in its true beauty and dignity
except after all external constraints, both of law and
public opinion, have been removed. She holds that its
essence consists in the voluntary choice of the parties
concerned, and that it is somehow degraded by being
legally safeguarded. I hold, on the contrary, that there
is no conflict or incongruity between perfect law and
perfect freedom, and that men and women cannot
suffer in the finest and most delicate aspects of their

mutual relations by having their ideal expressed and to some extent maintained by the general will of the community.

It is necessary, however, to distinguish clearly between an absolute ideal and the extent to which it is justifiable or expedient to impose that ideal upon people by law. The great error of the Catholic Church was its omission to draw this distinction. It would have escaped much scandal if it had sought to attain its ideal purpose by education instead of coercion. The High Church party in England and America is to-day imperilling its moral influence through falling into the same mistake. I am decidedly of opinion that in a more enlightened age divorce will be as completely obsolete as duelling is to-day in England. But I do not hold that such a state of things can or should be brought about by legal coercion. So far as the law is concerned, divorce should remain possible. Certainly nobody can defend the grotesque injustice of the English law, which deliberately restricts divorce to the rich and denies it to the poor, and permits it to the man for only one cause of offence, whereas a woman cannot obtain it for less than two causes, the second of which — cruelty — even in the wide definition given to it by "judge-made law," is peculiarly difficult to prove. Nor can any well-wisher of society contemplate without grave dissatisfaction the anarchic condition of American law on the subject. Divorce is here granted far too freely, and for far too many causes.

Owing, moreover, to the differing laws of different States, the absurd situation can and sometimes does arise, that a man or woman is legally married in one State and at the same time liable in another to a charge of bigamy. The immediately necessary reform in America is that there should be one uniform national law of divorce throughout the Union, and that such a law should curtail the number of grounds upon which the marriage tie may be dissolved. I will not attempt to formulate an exhaustive category of the permissible grounds, but the list should not extend far beyond the following: (1) Adultery (with the right of remarriage to both parties, but with such full publicity in the matter of names and facts that it would be impossible for the guilty party to remarry without the new wife or husband knowing the circumstances); (2) incurable insanity — the law specifying, however, in rigid terms, the circumstances which shall justify the conclusion that the insanity is incurable; (3) incurable drunkenness — subject to the same stipulation; (4) a prison conviction of either party for seven years or more; (5) the sterility of the union after five years, provided both parties concur in the demand. To grant divorce in this last case at the request of only one party would involve the possibility of hideous injustice to the other.

My reasons for opposing divorce on the ground of "incompatibility of temper" I shall have occasion to state partially at a later stage of the argument.

But what, it may be asked, becomes of the ideal of lifelong monogamy if the marriage bond is to be legally dissoluble on so many grounds? I answer that the law is not the only agency which may bring about an elevation of social standards, and that there are many reforms which a wise statesmanship will seek to effect by extra-legal methods. No law can be effectively enforced unless its principles be such as command the voluntary and unconstrained allegiance of the mass of the public. By passing measures which are not intended to be practised, or which public ignorance and hostility render unenforceable, no good is done, but rather the great harm of destroying men's respect for law and for the ideals it attempts to actualize. Hence arises the hard fact that in Roman Catholic countries there is just as much of the *thing* divorce (under other names) as among Protestant nations, and laxity of sexual life is notoriously not less prevalent among Catholic peoples than elsewhere. On the other hand, a general rise in the level of public opinion, and the consequent widening of the range of its censures, will frequently produce reform so rapidly and effectually as to render legislation superfluous.

An interesting illustration is afforded by the analogous case of excessive drinking. A hundred years ago in England, it was consistent with the canons of good taste and social propriety for the gentlemen at a dinner-party to finish the evening under the table. Even among members of the clerical profession the standard was scarcely higher than for the laity, and many un-edifying anecdotes are preserved of the "two-bottle orthodox." To-day, such conduct would result in social ostracism for any man, no matter how exalted his station in life, who dared to practise it. Yet in the promotion of this immense reform, legislation has had no share. So far as the law is concerned, a man is still free to get drunk every night in the week. The amelioration has been effected entirely by public opinion, which has changed in response to the growth of knowledge and the deepening of refinement. The vinous Pickwickians and Wardles, whom Dickens was able to portray as entirely acceptable members of society, would not to-day be tolerated anywhere save in the most degraded substratum of the populace, and even here they would be constantly censured for conduct which good society a hundred years ago accepted as a matter of course.

My hope and faith is that divorce will be got rid of by a strictly analogous process. While it remains legally possible, it will be rendered socially impossible, by reason of a growth of knowledge and foresight which will make the blunders that to-day lead to divorce inexcusable except in the very rarest cases. Our scientific knowledge of the facts relating to the union of the sexes is to-day greater than ever before, and is constantly increasing. We know, with almost quantitative exactness, the conditions under which certain diseases reappear in successive generations.

Where quantitative knowledge fails, we know approximately the dangers to be apprehended from the mating of persons among whose ancestry certain defects have appeared. We know, moreover, that the old assertion, "a reformed rake makes the best husband," is a hideously dangerous falsehood. This growing knowledge is being thrown into forms in which it can safely be imparted to young people of both sexes, so early in life that it cannot fail to influence even those non-rational impulses which awaken as maturity is approached.

The effect of such education will be not so much to provoke a painful clash between reason and inclination, as to prevent inclination itself from taking a dangerous direction. We grossly underestimate the extent to which the so-called blind impulses of human nature can be guided and controlled by ideational forces. We forget the plain and obvious fact that these impulses hardly ever canalize themselves except in directions generally sanctioned by public opinion. For example, as Sir Francis Galton pointed out in his first plea for eugenics, there is never any difficulty among primitive communities in maintaining the most rigorous tribal laws regarding marriage. Members of exogamous communities seldom fall in love with persons of their own kindred or totem; people in endogamous tribes rarely feel any disposition to marry outside the limits of their own community. Among ourselves, even, it is noteworthy that the sexual impulse almost invariably follows the lines laid down by convention and social expectation. A workingman almost never falls in love with a woman of the so-called upper class. A rich man hardly ever feels impelled to marry a woman of the people. When a "lady," technically so-called, marries her butler or elopes with her chauffeur, the most democratic onlooker finds himself (or more frequently herself) adjudging her to be mad — thereby unconsciously testifying that the sexual impulse not only normally is but *ought* to be canalized within rigid limits of educational and general cultural similarity, these being the necessary conditions of permanent mutual congeniality and common interest.

There is, of course, the ghastly fact of prostitution, involving a great deal of illicit intercourse between men of the wealthy class and outcast women; but nobody would confuse this with the discriminating selection and individualized affection which leads to marriage. The impulse which seeks its satisfaction in the brothel is the merely animal one, which has no relation to the individuality of its object.

These considerations suffice to show how comparatively easy it will be, by means of judiciously forewarning and forearming the young man and the maiden, to avert those tragic blunders which to-day are rectified, hardly less tragically, in the divorce court. Statute law need not necessarily have any part in the process. When once the teaching, called to-day by the unpleasant and unsatisfactory name of "sex hygiene," is given as it should be given, — that is, by parents, or, failing them, by teachers who impart to the lessons the spirit of awe and reverence which we associate with religion, — we may be certain that there will be created in the young such a wise alertness to secure their own lifelong well-being, and to promote the sanity, efficiency and virility of the future race, that the number of tragic failures resulting in divorce will be reduced almost to the vanishing-point. And when it has become practically inexcusable for people to marry without sufficient knowledge of one another, and of the probable consequences of a given union to themselves and to their offspring, it will be perfectly just for society to visit upon divorcees, of both sexes, the same heavy censures and penalties that it visits to-day upon the drunkard.

Let us now turn, however, to the indictment against marriage brought by Miss Key. I have quoted above the summary of her case against it from page 290 of "Love and Marriage." As we have seen, she holds marriage itself responsible for "the coarsest sexual habits, the most shameless traffic, the most agonising soul-murders, the most inhuman cruelties, and the grossest infringements of liberty that any department of modern life can show." These and other horrors, be it observed, she declares that *marriage has produced*, and is still producing. Here, however, she overlooks a discrimination which is absolutely essential to all intelligent sociological thinking. She argues in terms

of the ancient fallacy of *post hoc ergo propter hoc*.
These disgusting circumstances arise *after* marriage,
and Miss Key at once infers that they arise *because
of* marriage. Such a process of reasoning is at once
refuted by the fact that in the majority of marriages
these things never happen at all. They cannot, therefore, be necessary results of marriage, else they would
arise in every case. There must be some defect of
character or circumstance in the persons to whom
they do happen.

If fifty men, for example, are exposed to the midday
sun, and two of them get sunstroke, it would obviously
not be true to say that the sun's heat was a necessary and inevitable cause of sunstroke. If it were, how
could the forty-eight escape? It must be evident that
the sunstroke is caused by the conjuncture between
some weakening predisposition in the victims and the
rays to which they are exposed. If that weakness
could have been remedied beforehand, their exposure
to the sun would not have resulted in their disease.

It is a sound general rule that no human institution
is to be blamed for evils associated with it, unless it
can be demonstrated that the institution is itself the
cause of the evils, and therefore that its abolition
would be their cure. For example, in this country the
republican form of government has been, and still is,
associated with every description of vile and humiliat-
ing political corruption. Under it, offices have been
bought and sold, public servants have shamelessly

subordinated their patriotism to their pocket-books, and made the pretence of working for the common weal a mere mask for dishonest self-aggrandizement. Tenth-rate instead of first-rate men have been attracted to the public service, and it is still notoriously exceptional to find a politician who is also a gentleman. Indeed, the very title "politician" in America (alone among English-speaking nations) is almost equivalent to an insult; and to say of any piece of public work that "there is too much politics in it," is synonymous with saying that it has been exploited by dishonest persons for selfish ends.

Now, these faults have been seized upon by some European advocates of aristocracy or despotism as furnishing a conclusive condemnation of democracy. But in America, so far as I am aware, nobody has ever been foolish enough to suppose that these incidental vices of the political system are due to the fact that the United States is a republic, or that they could be extirpated by changing to a monarchical or aristocratic form of government. Everybody here is aware that the faults are not inherent in democracy, but only adherent to it. They arise from defects of character and low moral standards in the professional political class, and they will certainly be got rid of the moment the people in general cease to be obsessed by that mad craze for personal enrichment which makes them neglect their public responsibilities. Already there has been marked improvement, and the spread of woman suffrage is advancing that improvement with tremendous speed.

The same reasoning which distinguishes between corruption as an incident of democracy, and democracy as a cause of corruption, ought also to be applied to marriage, and indeed to every field of human interest. If in any given case it can be shown that admitted evils can be cured without abolishing the institution they contaminate, or, conversely, that the abolition of that institution would still leave the evils unremedied, then the institution itself is clearly not to blame. Now, even Mr. Shaw has discovered (through studying Brieux's play "Les Hannetons") that the evils he complains of in marriage can be developed in a tenfold worse form in illicit unions. Where a passionately jealous man or woman desires to monopolize the affections and attentions of a partner whose fidelity is secured by no legal tie, their relations become a source of mutual exasperation more hellish than any other human connection. The consciousness that there is no law or public opinion to sanction and uphold their fiercely asserted claim exacerbates the jealousy which arises from the lust of possession; and such degrading horrors could only be multiplied by setting people "free," as Miss Key's proposals would necessarily do, to enslave themselves anew upon every vagrant whim.

In short, the tacit assumption running throughout "Love and Marriage," and most other books of its kind, is not merely that marriage is the cause of the evils complained of, but that its abolition would be their cure; and this assumption is flatly contradicted by facts of experience within the knowledge of everybody.

A second presupposition of Miss Key's book is one that one feels a certain difficulty in criticizing. The difficulty arises from the fact that she merely states, without troubling to prove or defend, a position which to her is clearly self-evident, but which to her readers sounds like a frantic absurdity. This position — so obvious, apparently, to Miss Key — is that love and marriage are antithetical and mutually exclusive; that is to say, she holds that where there is marriage there cannot be love, and where there is love there cannot be marriage. She expresses this position in the following words: —

> The import of the moral controversies which now arise with increasing frequency is *the examination of the relatively higher value for real sexual morality of marriage or love.*[1]

I hasten to explain that the italics are Miss Key's. I could not myself hit upon any typographical device emphatic enough to express the overwhelming astonishment which her words create in my mind. If she means what she says, I am merely bewildered; if she means something else, I confess myself unable to divine what it can be. Here is an antithesis which has no shadow of a fact in heaven or earth to justify it. One

[1] *Love and Marriage*, p. 11.

might as well discuss "the relatively higher value for morality" of houses or domestic edifices, or the merits of bonnets as contrasted with coverings for the head. Yet this is no mere slip of expression on Miss Key's part. The antithesis she here sets up is presupposed throughout the entire course of her argument; so much so that the book might just as well be called "Love *or* Marriage" as "Love *and* Marriage." She is seriously convinced that these two things cannot coexist. She has somehow succeeded in overlooking the monumental fact that in most cases they are synonymous. She really does not know that most people get married because they love each other, and then obstinately go on loving each other, in spite even of the fact that they are married. She is not aware that this is a rule so universal that the only exceptions to it are degenerates or grown-up spoiled children.

If — to hazard a wild conjecture — if Miss Key really means that the issue is between so-called free love and marriage, this would only demonstrate how inveterately she thinks of marriage as consisting merely in the external legal bond. As a matter of fact, however, her own ideal of free love — that is, a connection which, though untrammelled, is to remain lifelong and exclusive — is itself the very definition of marriage, which is constituted between the two persons by their own free and final selection of each other, and is not created, but only ratified, by the civil or ecclesiastical ceremony. She can scarcely mean that children born in wedlock, but not "of love," are inferior to children born of a passionate love, whether within marriage or without; for she admits[1] that we have no data which could give any scientific warrant to the popular assumption to this effect.

The next error which we discover in Miss Key's argument discloses that blindness to moral distinctions of which I have ventured to accuse her. It is, briefly, the notion that things immoral in themselves can be made moral by legal sanction, and that the ethical quality of a given form of conduct can be changed by changing its name. This is a serious criticism, and yet I cannot but feel that her book fully justifies it. I will submit two instances of the deficiency to the reader's judgment.

On page 111 she writes :—

... Free love among the upper class — as among the lower class — will, it is true, contribute to the abolition of prostitution, but not to the exaltation of mankind through a greater love, a higher morality.

Free love will contribute to the abolition of prostitution. Undoubtedly it will contribute to the abolition of the word, and this will satisfy many; for, as Pascal says, "Le monde se paie de mots, peu approfondissent les choses." Or, to put it in a phrase more generally familiar, "Man does not live by bread alone, but principally by catch-words." But for one who pierces through words to facts, it is difficult to see how the

[1] *Love and Marriage*, p. 166.

abolition of prostitution can be effected by calling the same thing something else. What are the distinguishing marks of prostitution, if not cohabitation regardless of duty, terminable at pleasure, and transferable at will? I shall, of course, be told that the essence of prostitution is the fact that indulgence is bought and sold — that the outcast woman does this thing merely for money. I admit that the correction is warranted by some of the present-day facts. Yet if, as eminent medical and other scientific authorities are now telling us, there are many women who take to this life not from unqualified pecuniary need, but from preference, then the discrimination cannot be maintained, in view of the fact that such women are by universal consent classed as prostitutes. It is, moreover, as we have seen, a part of Miss Key's argument that the woman who practises free love is, when she becomes a mother, to receive monetary support from the community, both for herself and for her child. I cannot, then, conclude otherwise than that Miss Key does here display the lack of moral discrimination which I have ventured to charge against her. She does seriously propose to abolish this horrible evil by giving it legal sanction under a fresh name. In so far as the causation of prostitution is economic, there is, of course, no evidence that "free love" can even contribute towards its abolition.

It is indeed true that the whole of society to-day shows a moral blindness to the facts regarding prostitution far more serious than Miss Key's. Wrath and contempt are visited exclusively upon the outcast class of women, and the men whose patronage is responsible for their position go practically unscathed by public condemnation. The fact that every so-called fallen woman represents an indefinite number of men, who equally deserve the epithet "fallen," is seldom taken into consideration. The first step towards a true moral estimate of the situation must consist in seeing and saying clearly that society ought to take exactly the same attitude towards the fallen man that it takes towards the fallen woman. By this I mean, to put it in plain language, that if society ostracizes her it should ostracize him. If society invites him to dinner, it should invite her. If society is willing to marry its daughters to him, it should be equally willing — like Gilbey in "Fanny's First Play" — to marry its sons to her.

The second instance of defective moral vision is analogous to the first. At the commencement of her chapter on "Free Divorce," Miss Key speaks of "the desire of the present day to abolish adultery by means of free divorce." With this desire she clearly sympathizes and thinks it possible to comply. She proceeds to explain how, in her judgment, it should be met: —

> The true line of development will quite certainly be this: that divorce will be free, depending solely upon the will of both parties or of one, maintained for a certain time.

She also, in the name of the new morality, questions whether all adulterers

> in their innermost consciousness, really feel themselves to be sinners. The need which impelled them was perhaps so imperious that it justified them before their own conscience in choosing a lesser evil in preference to a greater.

Here it is best to express one's dissent in plain language, by stating that, if Miss Key's proposal were adopted, the only thing that would be abolished would be the word "adultery." The thing would remain, and would be ethically exactly what it is to-day. The idea that a statute can turn immorality into morality, or that the heinousness of a sin lies in its name, and can be eradicated by rebaptizing it, is one of those fundamental and widespread moral blindnesses which sometimes tempt one to despair of the spiritual advance of humanity. It is exactly as if men should be distressed by the prevalence of theft in our time, and should seriously propose to rid society of it by calling stealing business, and the thief a financier. This, of course, is what we very often do; but in connection with property, though our moral insight may be dim, our sense of humour enables us to see through the verbal jugglery.

Consider, for example, the instance that I cited at the outset, of a man who divorced his wife, united himself to a new partner, divorced her in turn, and returned to his wife. That man certainly got a certificate from some official of the law to sanction each of the steps he took. My contention, however, is that this precaution on his part did not lessen, by any jot or tittle, the immorality of his conduct. *Unless the grounds for a divorce are ethically satisfying, altogether apart from their legality,* the divorce is a crime, no matter how many statutes sanction it; and the subsequent union cannot be made other than adulterous by all the priests or magistrates in Christendom. Judging the case, therefore, upon its facts, I do not hesitate to declare that there was no moral difference between the conduct of this rich man and the practice of those men in the working class who desert and betray their wives, and afterwards return to them, without seeking to narcotize their consciences or hoodwink their neighbours by means of a legal sanction. I do not deny that, in some cases, conduct, otherwise moral in itself, may become immoral if practised in defiance of a statute law. This is a large question, upon which I need not here enter. But conduct immoral in itself can never become moral through being legalized.

We turn now to another, and a still more radical error of Miss Key and her school, — an error born of that anarchistic and atomistic individualism which is the real creed of many who imagine themselves Socialists. It is the idea, perpetually assumed and frequently stated in overt terms throughout this book of Ellen Key's, that happiness or unhappiness in marriage is a mere blind fatality and finality, entirely unrelated to, and independent of, the will of the parties concerned. She argues as though love were a thing like measles, which you catch through sheer bad luck, and often through no carelessness of your own, and which may presently pass away, either through or in spite of the efforts of the doctor. The moment the disease is gone, you are to be free to snap any connection which you have formed while under its influence. This is the great new morality of love *versus* marriage, — a new morality which in Miss Key's mind is entirely distinct from the old immorality, though probably few others will be able to fathom the distinction. She expresses herself in these unmistakable terms: —

> As soon as love is admitted as the moral ground of marriage, it will be a necessary consequence that he who has ceased to love, should be allowed a moral as well as a legal right to withdraw from his marriage, if he chooses to avail himself of this right.[1]

Notice, incidentally, how Miss Key's queer notion of morality peeps out through this statement. A man is to be *allowed* a moral right. That is to say, a moral right is a mere convention, and, as such, can be given or withheld by society. To those of us who hold that moral distinctions are embedded in the nature of things, in such wise that they can neither be created nor destroyed by any authority, the idea naturally seems fantastic. A man may, indeed, be permitted or denied the *exercise* of a moral right, but, as regards the

[1] *Love and Marriage*, pp. 290–91.

right itself, he either has it or has it not, and it can neither be given to nor taken from him.

But the radical error, illustrated in the typical sentence which I have just quoted, goes far deeper than this. It is the error involved in the whole modern practice of divorce for so-called "incompatibility of temper." It is the notion that a man's or a woman's own will and character have no part in determining the happiness or the unhappiness of a union. We take it for granted that, when a marriage is uncongenial, the parties merely *find* it so; we do not entertain, even in order to reject it, the idea that they may possibly have *made* their union unsatisfactory to themselves, or that any self-discipline on their part could make it satisfactory.

In this connection I may deal with the objection, which must have arisen in the minds of some readers, that "incompatibility of temper" did not figure in my list of causes for which divorce should be allowed. I reserved my criticism on this head because I wished to deal with it where it logically arises in the consideration of Miss Key's argument. I am opposed to divorce on this ground for two reasons: first, because if people's tempers are really so incompatible as to make their lifelong companionship intolerable, they can, and therefore ought to, know this in time to prevent their union. And, secondly, because such incompatibility as can remain entirely concealed before marriage, cannot possibly be so great but that it may be overcome and harmonized after marriage, by means of proper self-discipline and true grasp of the idea of duty.

It is noteworthy that we never think of admitting the principle involved in divorce for incompatibility in any other of the relations of life. No soldier would be pardoned for deserting from the army on the ground that he found his temper hopelessly incompatible with that of his comrades and his officers. No party to a business contract would be absolved from observing its terms upon any such consideration. These analogies are indeed inadequate, but only because marriage is so overwhelmingly important that no other human relation is comparable to it in significance. Yet no other connection in life, except the one inexpressibly significant and important one, is mankind willing to sunder on such a ground! Indeed, even in the case of blood relations, we seldom or never hear of people repudiating one another, *coram populo*, for any such reason. Parents and children, brothers and sisters, may have their family quarrels, and may separate temporarily — a course which is frequently wise and necessary also in the case of married people. But they are hardly ever foolish enough to declare that the differences of taste, interest and inclination between them are so great that they will never meet again or suffer society to recognize their relatedness; and when they do so, we can almost always see that — as in Schopenhauer's case — it is their own preventable perversity which is responsible.

This notion, that he or she who has ceased to love must be given a moral and legal right to withdraw from marriage, is a notion which simply denies the existence of duty, except in the narrowest self-regarding sense of the term — Miss Key's wonderful sense, in which "real selfishness . . . is one with real morality." [1] The modern free-lover is unwilling to admit that the claim of duty can pass beyond the mere conscious self-direction of the individual. He thinks that, whether a man is truly aware or not of those real organic needs of his personal and social nature which give content to the imperative of conscience, he is, nevertheless, to submit to no guidance or command from outside authorities, even though they know more truly than he what is really necessary for him and for the common life. This is a doctrine which would leave a conscientious burglar to his own devices, and prohibit, as unwarrantable tyranny, any interference by society with a sweating employer of child labour, or with the patrons of gambling dens. If, in the one department of a man's conduct which is fraught with the most serious import to society, he is to be wholly unamenable to law or public opinion, — if here the needs of the community give it no right to interfere, — how can any lesser social exigency be held to warrant either compulsion or restraint?

Those, however, who take the view that duty is something more than what a man consciously wants to

[1] *Love and Marriage*, p. 126.

do, and is indeed the sovereign and unconditional law of nature and reason, will have a clue guiding them to the exposure not only of the fallacy which we have just laid open, but of several other errors of the free-love school. One of these is the notion, always implied and frequently affirmed in their arguments, although sometimes verbally contradicted, that marriage is wholly or mainly a means to the individual happiness of those who enter upon it. Miss Key, of course, contends repeatedly that much more than this is involved; she contradicts herself, however, by claiming again and again that a marriage may be dissolved if it fails to secure this. Upon what other principle, indeed, could one justify divorce at the request of either party to a marriage, without inquisition into the reasons for the demand? The plain fact is that individual happiness cannot be either guaranteed or maintained by any human arrangement whatever. The securing of personal happiness, moreover, is not the true end of life; indeed, the claim of duty frequently begins to assert itself only when happiness is irretrievably lost. He who enjoys happiness is getting not what he deserves, but an ~~uncovenanted~~ bonus added to the dividend of life. He or she who makes the pursuit of happiness the dominant end of existence, is chasing a will-o'-the-wisp. The true end of life for the individual is perfection of character. This is attainable only in and through the service of all, and the subordination of self-centred desire to the claims of that higher selfhood, which is co-extensive and identical with the universal human trend towards the actualization of the moral ideal.

The right to renounce marriage because of unhappiness would logically involve the right to commit suicide for the same reason. He who thinks his claim to happiness so unchallengeable that he feels free to renounce wife and child in order to secure it, would surely also plead a right to cast away his own life, and his allegiance to the general life, for the same cause. This logical extension of the doctrine displays its monstrousness. Who are we that we should repudiate the universe because it will not devote itself to securing our petty pleasures and happinesses?

Akin to this is a still further ethical blunder, involved in the perpetual reiteration throughout Miss Key's book of the word "right." We are for ever hearing of the *right* to marriage, the *right* to divorce, the *right* to motherhood. The whole theory involves a looking at life through the wrong end of the telescope. We human beings have only such rights as are involved in and deducible from our duties. Debtors as we are to the world for more than we ever can repay, our only rights are those conditions necessary for the discharge, to the utmost of our powers, of the inexhaustible claims of humanity upon us. And marriage, like every other great social ordinance, is instituted not primarily to secure our happiness, but to enable us to discharge our duty, in the matter of the perpetuation and spiritual development of the human species, with the possible maximum of racial efficiency. Happily, it also secures incidentally the possible maximum of personal satisfaction in well-doing; but inasmuch as this is not its first or most important function, it is not to be condemned when it fails to secure this, provided it does attain its primal and paramount ends.

From this standpoint, I contend that every one of the evils complained of in marriage by Miss Ellen Key is demonstrably due not to marriage as an institution, but to other causes, all of which are removable without tampering with marriage, and every one of which, unless specially dealt with, would manifest itself under any other system of sex relations which the wit of man could devise. Inasmuch, then, as we still should have to grapple with these other causes of mischief, after we had rooted up the monogamic principle, it is surely advisable that we should seek to begin by getting rid of them, and reserve our criticism of marriage itself until we see how it works out, after they have been abolished.

These extraneous causes of evil, for the consequences of which marriage is unfairly condemned, may be compendiously summed up under three headings: (1) ignorance, leading to heedlessness in marriage selection, and consequent disasters after marriage; (2) defects of personal character, which we wrongly treat as finalities, instead of insisting that the individuals, because they could cure them, must be held responsible for them; and (3) bad economic conditions, legal in-

equalities and false social standards. With the first two
of these I have perhaps dealt at sufficient length. Let
us pass to the third, by way of a preliminary analysis
of another false moral principle, widely prevalent in
the modern world.

That false principle is the tendency of men and
women, when they discover a conflict between ideals
and facts, to surrender their ideals instead of attacking
and overthrowing the facts. One could illustrate this
by endless examples; I will content myself with one or
two. A few years ago, I saw in England, on the adver-
tisement placard of a weekly paper, the words "Should
Shop Assistants Marry?" The article turned out to be
an analysis of the conditions under which shop assistants live — the long hours of labour, the wretched
wages, insufficient even for the decent support of a
single individual, and the cramped and inadequate
housing to which these wages condemn them; and the
whole argument was made to issue in the conclusion,
quite frankly accepted by the writer, that, in view of
their conditions, shop assistants ought not to marry.
I can scarcely think of a more dramatic exemplifica-
tion of the fact I have alleged. The question which
any unhypnotized man would ask, is not "Should
shop assistants marry?" but rather, "Should any
human being submit to conditions which make it
practically impossible for him or her to marry?" Instead of asking this obvious and natural question,
however, we submit like cowards to the mere exist-

ing fact, thereby implicitly assenting to the fatalistic mythology of economic determinism, which teaches that outward circumstance alone controls man. It is as if we should argue that because legs are inconvenient in automobiles (and they are abominably so in most of them!), we ought to amputate the legs.

Lest this parallel should seem too grotesque, let me hasten to add that here in America we do actually resign ourselves to a practical conclusion scarcely less absurd. In every American city that I know of, it is found that ordinary comfort and decency in the public street-cars are incompatible with large profits to the corporations which own the franchises. This being the case, instead of saying (as a civilized nation would do) that the corporations must be content with smaller profits, we blandly acquiesce in the perpetuation of overcrowding, discomfort, filth and disease-laden air in our public conveyances. If anybody objects to this, the answer — given even by women, whose sense of personal dignity and decency is daily outraged by the intolerable conditions — is that it is impossible to provide seats for all in cities so huge as New York, Philadelphia or Chicago. To which the reply is that in Europe the problem has been solved in cities still larger; and that the alleged impossibility will vanish the moment the American public resolves to make the pecuniary interests of corporations altogether secondary to that public convenience the service of which alone justifies their existence.

The principle involved in our attitude towards those social conditions which make marriage difficult for men and women during the best years of life is exactly similar. Because professional men are poorly paid during those years when they ought to be perpetuating the sacred gift of life, of which they are the trustees and depositaries, we assent to their not marrying, instead of abolishing the conditions which prevent their doing so. Because the unmarried woman, if she is fairly well paid for her work, would have to sacrifice certain comforts and luxuries by accepting the highest functions to which destiny calls her, we think it entirely natural that she should prefer pleasure to duty. Instead of regarding it as necessary, or even as possible, so to change the economic conditions that she need lose nothing of value, we accept the brute economic facts as final, and begin to talk of abolishing marriage and giving the woman a right to motherhood apart from it.

Yet how can anyone fail to see that the abolition of marriage and the sanctioning of parenthood in the case of unmarried persons would leave the economic difficulty exactly where it is to-day? Those conditions which militate against marriage would be just as inimical to parenthood without marriage as within it. If people are too poor to maintain a home, and to beget and bring up children on the basis of legally sanctioned monogamic union, they are equally too poor to have homes and children on the free-love basis. After all, it is the maintenance of the home and the nurture of the children that cost the money, and therefore constitute the difficulty; and the abolition of marriage without change in the economic conditions would not be even the beginning of a solution of the fundamental problem. How, then, can we dream (as free-love theorists seem to do) that the difficulty arises from the fact that the parents are bound by a legally sanctioned tie, which in normal cases is indissoluble? The idea that the removal of this tie will produce a reform is a part of that deep-seated confusion of thought which blames an institution for evils manifested in connection with it, under the false impression that they spring from it.

But the world to-day is much too ready to make economic conditions the scapegoat for its derelictions of social duty. We hear many men complain, for example, that they cannot afford to marry and face the expense of a home and children, when what they really mean is that they cannot afford the particular kind of home which the standard of social expectation in their set prescribes as necessary. I recently talked with a gentleman who bitterly bemoaned these hard conditions. He was a rich man, but had built up his fortune by his own exertions. He explained that he had been unable to marry until he was nearly forty, at which time he united himself with a lady of approximately equal age. He told me that it was the standing grief of both of them that they had no children and could never have any. But, he added, the thing was inevitable, for from the time he was twenty-five until he was approaching forty, he had not earned enough to marry on. I ventured to inquire what his income had been when he was twenty-six or twenty-seven. "Twenty dollars a week," he replied. Hereupon I put a second question: "Are you not aware that at least seventy or eighty per cent. of the families in this country are being run, and run reasonably well, on twenty dollars a week or less, even to-day, when the purchasing power of twenty dollars is far smaller than it was in your time?"

This is the hard fact! A man and woman can live, if they have common sense and practical wisdom, and ethical standards instead of merely conventional ones, on a small income such as my friend specified. True, they cannot have automobiles or season tickets for the opera, but they can have "the things that are more excellent" — the things without which luxuries speedily become a sickening disappointment. The story has recently been told [1] of a middle-class family in one of the Eastern cities, where the man had for many years been an accountant, enjoying a fairly good salary, which, like most middle-class people, he and his wife had regularly spent, usually on things of no real value. In middle life he lost his situation, had no savings to fall back upon, and was speedily face to face with destitution. In this predicament, it occurred to him

[1] *One Way Out: A Middle-Class New Englander Emigrates to America.* By William Carleton. (Boston: Small, Maynard. Eighth issue, 1913.)

— an American by birth and ancestry, who had lived all his life in his own country — that he might try the plan of "emigrating to America." He suggested this to his wife, and found her willing to co-operate in the experiment. He removed to another quarter of the city, took a cheap flat in the working-class district, and accepted a job at nine dollars a week in an Italian labouring gang. Small as his income was, he found himself able to save out of it, now that he had cut himself free from the expensive idolatries of his middle-class life. Having now leisure in his evenings, for the first time in his life, he learned the Italian language, in order that he might be able to converse with his co-workers, and went to the night school, where he learned the higher branches of his trade. His superior education, coupled with his business training, enabled him speedily to rise in his new trade to the position of a foreman, and subsequently he became a contractor, and built up a prosperous business.

This is an illustration of the real point, that what we commonly mistake for poverty is not really poverty at all, but slavery to preconceived notions dictated by our social set. A man who has the rare and terrific courage to *appear* poorer than the bulk of the persons with whom he associates, can be much better off than the cowardly mass of us, who, with larger incomes, surrender unconditionally to that sordid tradesmen's conspiracy which bids us deify appearances. The great ends of life, the fundamental needs both of society and of our individual nature, are deliberately sacrificed on the altar of a tawdry, bourgeois respectability; and, having made the sacrifice, we plead our cowardice as its own justification. A sounder sense of the economic needs of man, and a clearer ethical idealism — into both of which things we shall speedily be forced by the ghastly consequences of our present practices — will drive us back to a true simplicity of life, which we shall find, as did the man whose case I have just epitomized, infinitely more satisfying than the life of vain display to which at present we suffer ourselves to be held in bondage.

All of which, however, is neither in intention nor in effect a defence of conditions as they are. I yield to no man in my economic radicalism; I am only anxious to distinguish between real poverty and imaginary, and to beat back the widespread hypocrisy which pleads impossibility where no impossibility exists, and denies that an educated man and woman can do what millions of people are already actually doing. Nor am I so impressed as many people are by the argument from economic insecurity. I admit that uncertainty as to the future is a good reason for circumspection and forethought; I deny that it justifies the avoidance of all risks. The cowardice which will take no chance of the possibility of future poverty — which will not marry until it is assured of a sufficient income in perpetuity — is to - day carried to entirely indefensible lengths. People overlook the added spur which responsibility gives to the spirit of enterprise. I have several times advised young people to make what are called rash marriages, and in every instance my imprudent counsel has been justified by results. The struggling young professional man, who induces the woman of his choice to share life with him, at once has tenfold the incentive of his bachelor confrère to the study and exertion which lead to professional advancement.

It is astonishing how speedily the increase of wealth, and the consequent raising of standards of social expectation in this country, have sapped the boasted spirit of the pioneer. Men and women whose grandparents were ready to defy hardships which to us are almost unimaginable, are unwilling to-day to face the possibility of having to substitute the pipe for the cigar or to dispense with supernumerary garments. This slavery to luxury is the most enervating disease that can attack a community. At a time when even artisans have at their command comforts and conveniences impossible to the European monarchs of a century ago, we find men and women afraid to marry, even when there is, practically speaking, no reasonable ground for fear that they will ever be in want of the necessaries of life. The removal of this fantastic nightmare, and of the hypnosis begotten of it, is at least as necessary as the reform of economic conditions.

It is entirely necessary that we should redistribute the wealth of the nation on the principle of social expediency, instead of, as at present, on the principle of every man for himself, and the devil take the common good. To pay the bachelor at the same rate as the father of a family, to tax the man who spends his whole income on himself at no higher rate than we tax the man who spends his income on a wife and children, is, socially speaking, insane. To settle questions of wages by what people can be forced to work for, instead of by what scientific knowledge shows to be necessary for civic and national efficiency, is an instance of individualistic barbarism which, to a future generation, will be unthinkable. To allow an employer to sponge upon private philanthropy and the public purse, by employing girls and women at wages which have to be supplemented from these other sources — thereby making the capitalist the real pauper — is, entirely apart from ethical considerations, an economic imbecility. Of all of these things we shall soon grow heartily ashamed, to such an extent that we shall sweep them away. Meantime, however, let us turn the searchlight on the dark spot in ourselves. Let us be certain that when we absolve ourselves from our most important social duties on the ground of their economic impossibility, it is a real impossibility that deters us, and not a mere figment of a bemused imagination.

I have reserved to the last, the examination of the most fundamental reason for opposing Miss Key's doctrine of free love. It is one which seems never to have occurred to her, or to Mr. Shaw or to George

Meredith. Yet to most of us it seems so self-evident and conclusive that we cannot understand how any serious thinker could come forward with revolutionary proposals without taking it into consideration. This fundamental objection is the fact that, when once the finality of marriage is abrogated, when law and custom sanction unions which to-day are branded as illicit, and a right to parenthood apart from marriage is conferred on men and women, the stability of every union would be menaced in such a fashion as to render life intolerable. For then every married man and woman would be as much a possible and legitimate object of sexual selection as unmarried men and women are to-day possible objects of marriage selection. It is curious how widely this patent fact is overlooked. One is always hearing married women, for example, expressing the most genuine and heartfelt sympathy for unmarried women. How shameful, they say, that So-and-So, who would make such an ideal mother, can have no chance of figuring in that capacity! If such women realized that the conferring of society's sanction on motherhood, under such circumstances, would make their own husbands legitimate objects of selection by the unmarried women as fathers for their children, the enormity of the consequences involved in the proposal would at once begin to dawn upon them. The thought of a state of society in which gentlemen could make love to their neighbours' wives without any censure by law or public opinion, and in which ladies could delicately hint their preference for the husbands of their friends, is too repellent to be seriously entertained. Yet this would be an inevitable consequence of such changes as those advocated by Miss Key and her school. One cannot tamper with the delicate equipoise of the fabric of practical morality without incurring the danger of overturning the entire system.

Hard cases constantly arise under our present organization. Most of these can, as I have shown, be got rid of without attacking the fundamental principle of lifelong monogamy. Yet to the end of time, under any conceivable system, cases of hardship must needs arise. It is vain to suppose that any human arrangement can secure immunity from misfortune, in a world whose forces are blind and indifferent to our fate. But the experience of mankind through the ages has not gone for nothing. Not without good cause has the general will decreed that the choice by men and women of each other must be irrevocable. For one tragedy which the free-love principle would avert, it would cause a hundred.

It is quite true that men and women to-day, and particularly men, by no means live up to the ideal embodied in the principle of lifelong monogamy. The cynic points to the notorious gap between profession and practice, and urges that this should be got rid of by squaring the ideal with the facts. Such a proposal, however, is childishly superficial. Bad as the facts are, low as is the level of actual conduct, things would be made worse and not better by lowering our standard. Moreover, the demand of monogamy is by no means an impossible one. The difficulty of continent celibacy and marital fidelity is grossly exaggerated. It is necessary to make high demands on human nature, not merely in order to bring out its best, but even to preserve it from utter degradation.

I have said of Miss Key (and the stricture is equally true of Mr. Shaw) that she thinks of marriage as consisting merely in the external legal tie that binds people together. This is the common presupposition of the whole of the modern free-love school. If they think at all of the old saying, "They twain shall be one flesh," they think of it as the expression of an arbitrary supernaturalistic dogma. They do not perceive that it is the statement of a self-evident natural fact. It does not so much declare what ought to be as describe what, in normal cases, actually happens in everyday experience. A man and woman, associated for years in the inexpressible intimacy of marriage, do actually, as a matter of simple truth, become one flesh. The relation between them is verily as indissoluble as that between themselves and their offspring. This was excellently expressed by Mr. George W. Smith, of the Philadelphia Bar, in an address given before the Ohio Bar Association in 1909: —

The status of matrimony may be stripped of its incidents by the municipal law, but no decree of any court, or act of legislature, can restore the natural status of one who has been married to that of one who never has been married. Life is full of finalities, and, as has been finely said, there is something tragic in everything that is final.[1]

Mr. Smith ought to have added that no decree of nullity pronounced by an ecclesiastical court can remove the effects of marriage. His statement is so true that, like the platitude with which this chapter commences, it sounds to our sophisticated ears paradoxical. The relation of husband and wife is so inherently infrangible that the sunderance of it by legal decree can be scarcely less tragic than the worst tragedy it is invoked to rectify. The closest ties of consanguinity are themselves derived from this relation, which we strangely enough imagine we can abrogate by a judicial sentence.

I may not conclude without alluding to one more point in the case against Miss Key, which could not be adequately dealt with save in a lengthy chapter; and I mention it merely that the reader may not suppose I had overlooked it. Sanity and virility demand that that impulse which leads to the union of the sexes should not be suffered to function out of relation to the entire hierarchy of human instincts, emotions and sentiments. It must be so correlated and systematized with all the other relations between man and woman, that the single person who satisfies the one desire shall

[1] Quoted by the Reverend Edwin Heyl Delk, D.D., in an article on "Divorce and Social Welfare," in the *Biblical World* for January, 1914.

harmonize with every aspect of the yearning for comradeship. The man or woman who *permits* the fleshly attraction to arise towards a succession of persons is on the way to insanity. A "scientific breeding of the human race" such as Mr. Shaw advocates — by allowing people "who have never seen each other before and never intend to see each other again" to have children (under certain definite conditions) "without loss of honour," would lead to the disappearance of the human race, or at least to the elimination from humanity of all that is distinctively human.

In other words, that union which is based solely on a sub-rational fascination is not worthy of the name of marriage. A true human union is one in which this primordial bond is co-ordinated with every other taste and interest in life. Nor is such harmony of the rational with the emotional by any means so rare or so difficult of attainment as is commonly supposed. Men and women are "masters of their fate" to a far greater extent than we ordinarily admit. Its mastery, however, necessitates severe self-discipline, and a constant vigilance in the adaptation of will to will and of mind to mind. Yet the necessity of such self-control and self-determination, instead of being a tragic hardship, is an indispensable element in moral education and character-building; and the fact that marriage calls for it is one of the strongest of all the reasons in favour of marriage.

CHAPTER VII

AMONG the world - wide literary reputations of our day, none is more thoroughly deserved than that of M. Maurice Maeterlinck. It is twenty-five years since his name was first trumpeted to the world by Octave Mirbeau, in a glowing article in the Paris "Figaro," entitled "A Belgian Shakespeare." Thanks to this perhaps over-generous appreciation, Maeterlinck "burst out into sudden blaze," and experienced the first flush of a popularity which has since grown more discriminating, but has nevertheless both deepened and widened with the years that have followed. His American admirers, for the most part, read him only in translation; yet inasmuch as they have the rare powers of Mr. de Mattos placed at their service in the humble but important function of translator, their loss is less than it would be under other circumstances. It remains, none the less, a loss; for one can never quite appreciate to the full the subtle quality of Maeterlinck's thought and imagination unless one has the aid of his very characteristic style. There is about his prose an ethereality akin to that of the atmosphere which broods over "Pelléas and Mélisande" and over "The Blue Bird."

This atmosphere, half intellectual, half imaginative, is the literary reflex of that temperamental quality denoted by the fashionable word of the moment: mysticism. Now, that word and the thing it signifies, because they happen at the moment to be the vogue, need to be saved from their friends more than in other times they may need to be rescued from their enemies. There is a fashion in philosophies as there is in dress, and popularization seems inevitably to involve vulgarization — using that term in its depreciatory sense. The truth is, the great public does not know a mystic when it sees one, and is accordingly dependent upon the information of reviewers, — as the tourist is commonly dependent on the asterisks of Baedeker to tell him which of a dozen pictures before his eyes is the masterpiece. Maeterlinck has received his label; we therefore rush to him to see what mysticism is. At the same time we neglect our greater homebred mystics, because our diurnal and hebdomadal oracles have either forgotten, or are themselves unaware, that several of the greatest mystics of the nineteenth century are to be found in the first rank of American literary men.

Emerson, the prince of modern mystics (whose so-called "transcendentalism" was, indeed, only a clumsier name for this very quality), is still sold, to be sure, by the cubic foot in pasteboard coffins, in our department stores; and it would be as incorrect not to have him enshrined upon one's shelves as it would be to be caught reading him. He is delivered over, bound hand and foot, to the manufacturer and purveyor of éditions-de-looks, and so unknown is he to our myriad devotees of "the latest thing" that they do not recognize his voice when it sounds from the gramophone records of later and lesser writers whom he has inspired.

Foremost among these latter is M. Maeterlinck, of whom it is no depreciation to say that, as a thinker, he is essentially unoriginal. His greatness is that of the poet. In this territory he has his own distinctive field. His thought, at its best, is but Emerson-and-water. No Emersonian, for example, could read " La Sagesse et la Destinée" without recognizing a body of doctrine with which he has long been familiar.

It is unfortunate that the public cannot dispense with labels. America, despite all its utilitarianism, is fundamentally the most idealistic, the most mystical, because the most intuitive, of modern nations; and this quality permeates the writing not alone of Emerson, but of several other of its poets and prophets whose renown is international, and who therefore (in accordance with precedent) are practically unhonoured in their own country. Whitman, for example, is a mystic to the core. The utterance of Holmes and Lowell is enriched by the same Vision Splendid. But because the public is familiar with the word mysticism rather than the thing, these men are abandoned to a cold-storage immortality. Such writers as Maeterlinck, who are the mere retailers of their inspiration, are credited with a solar instead of a lunar radiance, while the true luminaries are veiled in disastrous twilight.

All this, I repeat, is no depreciation of Maeterlinck and his kind. The retailer is as indispensable a functionary in the world of the spirit as he seems to be in that of commerce, and it does not lie in human power to discharge this function more exquisitely than does our Belgian poet. "The Blue Bird" is a perfect prism into which the white light pours, and from which it passes out with all its latent glories made visible to every eye. Its lesson is the eternal truth of mysticism. The children have revealed to them the inner meaning of all daily familiar things. They search through time and eternity, among the dead and among the unborn, in the kingdom of the past and the kingdom of the future, for "the great secret of things and of happiness." They end by finding it in their cottage — where it has been all the time.

Definitions, though dangerous, are indispensable; and we must attempt some approximate and working formula for mysticism, if only to shatter the prevalent confusion which makes it synonymous with mystification. No two things could really be more distinct than these, yet none could be more inextricably confounded in the mind of the devotee of fashion. Our definition, accordingly, may have its use, even though it serve only as a challenge to the label-worshipper. We shall

assert, therefore, that mysticism is the doctrine or the
spiritual attitude which *seeks the meaning of life in its
values rather than in its facts*. It is thus primarily voli-
tionalism as distinguished from intellectualism. It
sees that a scientific knowledge of the data and uniformities of the sense-world can never reveal to us the
secrets of reality. These are to be sought in the categories of good-and-bad, beautiful-and-ugly, rather than
in that of true-and-false. It does not in the least invalidate the sovereignty of truth, but it emphasizes
rather the truth-seeking impulse than the outer facts
to the discovery of which that impulse leads. Now,
because the will of man is the unique and solitary
source of all values whatsoever, mysticism seeks at
home for those answers to the eternal riddles which
science can only seek vainly abroad. Mysticism adopts
the standpoint of Protagoras, that "man is the measure of all things." The choir of heaven and furniture
of the earth depend upon the percipient and appraising
mind of humanity for their worth and meaning, even
if not for their existence. Inasmuch, then, as worth is
the supreme human category, mysticism endorses
unreservedly the great saying of Isidore: "Why dost
thou wonder, O Man, at the height of the stars or
the depth of the sea? Enter into thine own soul, and
wonder there."

Thus it happens that mysticism is the absolute opposite of dogmatism. It is incurious as to the unanswered and unanswerable questions which our theolo-

gies thrust into the foreground, making their guesses at them the basis of religious fellowship, and denying that a man can walk with confidence among the shadows, except he take their winking marsh-lights for his soul's guide.

From this high plane of mysticism, M. Maeterlinck has unfortunately descended in his latest volume.[1] He gives us, indeed, much thought on the subject of death that is full of interest and helpfulness. He tears away the grotesque veils and trappings which have concealed the true lineaments of the "dark Mother." But after this, he proceeds to humour that prying curiosity as to the fate of the individual after he has submitted to death's embrace, which the authentic mystic voice has always rebuked. He does not censure, as a mystic should, the vulgarity which betrays its own insecurity and lack of faith by peering into crystals, consulting the augurs and seeking news of the departed at the lips of trance-bound mediums, instead of in the surviving memorials of their human life and work. As M. Maeterlinck here fails us, let us revert to the high and searching words of his master: —

> Of immortality, the soul, when well employed, is incurious. It is so well that it is sure it will be well. It asks no questions of the Supreme Power. The son of Antiochus asked his father when he would join battle. "Dost thou fear," replied the King, "that thou only in all the army

[1] *Our Eternity.* By Maurice Maeterlinck. Translated by Alexander Teixeira de Mattos. (New York: Dodd, Mead & Co., 1913.)

wilt not hear the trumpet?" 'T is a higher thing to confide that, if it is best we should live, we shall live — 't is higher to have this conviction than to have the lease of indefinite centuries and millenniums and æons. Higher than the question of our duration is the question of our deserving. Immortality will come to such as are fit for it, and he who would be a great soul in future must be a great soul now. It is a doctrine too great to rest on any legend — that is, on any man's experience but our own. It must be proved, if at all, from our own activity and designs, which imply an interminable future for their play.[1]

"Higher than the question of our duration is the question of our deserving." There speaks the true prophet of mysticism. He who is concerned rather to deserve than to endure, and to be a great soul now rather than in some remote and uncontrollable future, is the truly regenerate man; and none such will ever be willing to waste in séance-rooms the time that is all too short for this higher and harder task.

Into the questions of the evidence for personal continuity which M. Maeterlinck raises, we shall not now follow him. Our present purpose is to study his teaching in regard to what has been called euthanasia — the doctrine, that is, that the sufferer whose end seems near shall have a right to be set free from the pangs of mortality by the action of the physician. His judgment on this point he sets out in the following paragraphs: —

[1] Emerson's essay on "Worship," in *The Conduct of Life*.

As science progresses, it prolongs the agony which is the most dreadful moment and the sharpest peak of human pain and horror, for the watchers, at least; for very often the consciousness of him whom death, in Bossuet's phrase, has "brought to bay" is already greatly dulled and perceives no more than the distant murmur of the sufferings which it seems to be enduring. All doctors consider it their first duty to prolong to the uttermost even the cruellest pangs of the most hopeless agony. Who has not, at the bedside of a dying man, twenty times wished and not once dared to throw himself at their feet and implore them to show mercy? They are filled with so great a certainty, and the duty which they obey leaves so little room for the least doubt, that pity and reason, blinded by tears, curb their revolt and recoil before a law which all recognize and revere as the highest law of man's conscience.

One day, this prejudice will strike us as barbarous. Its roots go down to the unacknowledged fears left in the heart by religions that have long since died out in the intelligence of men. That is why the doctors act as though they were convinced that there is no known torture but is preferable to those awaiting us in the unknown. They seem persuaded that every minute gained amid the most intolerable sufferings is snatched from the incomparably more dreadful sufferings which the mysteries of the hereafter reserve for men; and, of two evils, to avoid that which they know to be imaginary, they choose the real one. . . .

The doctors, on their side, say or might say that, in the present stage of science, two or three cases excepted, there is never a certainty of death. Not to support life to its last limits, even at the cost of insupportable torments, might be murder. Doubtless there is not one chance in a hundred thousand that the patient escape. No matter. If that chance exist which, in the majority of cases, will give but a few days, or, at the utmost, a few months of a life that will not be the real life, but much rather, as the Romans called it, "an extended death," those hundred thousand useless torments will not have been in vain. A single hour snatched from death outweighs a whole existence of tortures. . . .

A day will come when science will turn upon its error and no longer hesitate to shorten our woes. A day will come when it will dare and act with certainty. Once the doctor and the sick man have learned what they have to learn, there will be no physical nor metaphysical reason why the advent of death should not be as salutary as that of sleep.[1]

Against this eloquent and at first sight impressive plea for the right of the physical sufferer to be released, and consequently of the doctor to kill, there are many objections to be raised. These I shall divide for convenience into two classes. The first I shall call the objections of common-sense, the second the ethical objections. The division is, I agree, in the main arbitrary, and is resorted to only for convenience. Both sets of arguments are entitled to both labels; but those which I shall group under the distinctive title of ethical are those which do not spontaneously occur to the practical man, and are generally absent from discussions of the subject.

I would first draw attention to the interesting fact that the case for euthanasia in the abstract commends

[1] *Our Eternity*, pp. 19–25.

itself to many who, nevertheless, would find themselves unwilling to assent to it in any particular instance. On general grounds it seems so obvious, so rational and so humane that most of us would hesitate to reject it unqualifiedly. But if we actually find ourselves exceedingly reluctant to practise or to sanction, in some special case, a doctrine to which we have given our assent in the abstract, we must take account of that reluctance in ourselves as a datum in the problem, and re-examine the argument which had before seemed so convincing.

Several years ago, a lady was suffering from an incurable illness which made it impossible for her to leave her bed, or even to rise to a sitting position. She was what is called a Rationalist, and she sent for a number of prominent gentlemen whose views of religion were approximately the same as her own. These she consulted as to whether, under the circumstances, she was not entitled either to take her own life, or to have her irremediable suffering terminated by her doctors. At least two of the gentlemen whose counsel she sought had, in public utterances, endorsed the point of view which M. Maeterlinck has now set forth afresh. But neither of them was willing to accept the responsibility of assenting to the invalid lady's plea, although every canon of logical consistency demanded that they should do so. The pragmatic test proved too severe for them.

I cite this case, not in the least to condemn the gentlemen in question, but merely to reinforce the point I have just made. The fact that men who had publicly committed themselves to the doctrine that incurable sufferers have the right to death, yet hesitated to accord that right to the one particular sufferer who appealed to them, does, I think, show that when they assented to the general thesis, their sympathies travelled faster than their judgment. It is in the conviction that most men and women who agree with M. Maeterlinck are in the same position, that I venture now to re-examine the grounds of his doctrine. The result of such a procedure should be either to furnish us with valid reasons for rejecting the doctrine, or else so to reinforce it that we shall no longer hesitate to consent in practice to what we have assented to in theory.

Of the common-sense objections to which I have alluded, the first is that which M. Maeterlinck himself recognizes: "In the present stage of science, two or three cases excepted, there is never a certainty of death." This is a fact which has much more weight with the experienced physician than it commonly has with the laity. The public, as Mr. Bernard Shaw has reminded us, is far too ready to believe in the infallibility of the doctor; but the doctor, to do him justice, is very rarely such a fool as to believe in his own infallibility. He is more apt to say, as did Pius IX of his hot-headed adorers, "Questi infallibilisti mi faranno fallire." The opinions he utters are hedged about in his own mind with all sorts of qualifications and provisos, which he cannot make intelligible to the anxious relatives of his patient. What they want is a definite assurance, an unqualified yes or no. When he says, "I *think* your father will die," or, "I *believe* your sister will get better," he is understood to say, "I *know* your father will die," or, "*It is certain* that your sister will recover." The notorious fallibility of these prognostications, recognized in general by everybody, is forgotten by the anxious ones in connection with the case in which they are immediately interested.

Now if, when a doctor gives a patient up, he should proceed to end that patient's sufferings, it would never be possible afterwards to prove either that the patient would or that he would not have recovered. As illustrative cases have occurred in everybody's experience, I may be permitted to cite two from my own. A man suffering from an incurable disease was on two separate occasions, by two different doctors, given less than twenty-four hours to live. He died seven years later, having in the meantime never, indeed, been restored to full health, but having often been well enough to be up and doing. My second instance is that of a woman who, eighteen years ago, was declared to be dying of phthisis, and to have less than a week to live. She is alive to-day, in better health than she ever had before, and with no symptom of phthisis or any similar disease. It is perfectly possible that three or four doctors in consultation might have agreed on the verdicts to which I have referred, — although I gravely doubt whether any set of doctors would ever concur in such a judgment, if the responsibility of acting upon their conviction were imposed upon them. Suppose they had done so, however, in my second instance: the woman in question would simply have been cut off in the midst of her days, and her family would have been robbed of the joy and consolation of many years of her beneficent activity. When M. Maeterlinck says, "Doubtless there is not one chance in a hundred thousand that the patient escape," he expresses immensely more certitude than the competent doctor usually feels. Medical prophecies in such cases are generally the vaguest of guesswork, and the doctors (at least among themselves) admit that they are so. Medical science is extremely immature, and the factors in any given case are altogether too complicated to warrant a confident induction.

The second objection on the plane of common-sense is the undeniable possibility of the abuse of the power of life and death, by venal physicians acting in collusion with interested and unscrupulous relatives. If the right were given at all, it would have to be given to three or four doctors at most, acting upon their unanimous judgment. We know too much, however, of the blinding effect of self-interest even upon men's conscientious opinions, to place the issues of life and death in such hands. Witness, in the recent unsavoury case of the man Thaw, the flatly self-contradictory opinions as to his sanity expressed by the two sets of alienists — those retained in his interest, and those retained by the State. With perfectly shocking unanimity, his own mental experts declared him sane; with equal confidence the other side voted him insane. To decide when doctors disagree is proverbially difficult; experience also shows, however, that it would often be exceedingly dangerous to act when they do not disagree. It seems fairly probable that the average longevity of wealthy people would be materially decreased if their heirs had the right to authorize the administration of the quietus whenever three or four doctors could be found to concur in declaring recovery impossible. This statement may sound cynical, yet it is assuredly not devoid of a justifying basis in experience.

The third obvious objection is that to make doctors responsible for the termination of human suffering would inevitably undermine that sense of the sanctity of human life which is one of the most valuable of the hard-won conquests of civilization. It would increase the already exaggerated horror of mere physical suffering, and would place an appalling responsibility upon judgments biased by the contemplation of bodily pain. M. Maeterlinck's own words are here instructive: "Who has not, at the bedside of a dying man, twenty times wished and not once dared to throw himself at their [the doctors'] feet and implore them to show mercy?" But who, we may add, has not often had this feeling in connection with a patient who has subsequently recovered? The doctor to-day has law and public opinion to reinforce his resistance to such appeals. But if the law were on the side of the agonized lay onlookers, we cannot doubt that the doctor's judgment would often be overborne by their importunity.

It is interesting to note that the old indifference to the sanctity of life was rooted in insensitiveness to bodily and mental suffering. It would be strange if our developed sensibility to these things should lead finally to a recurrence of the very evil from which it has delivered us — if we should now be willing to sacrifice life from excessive horror of suffering, just as men in former times sacrificed it through an inadequate sensitiveness. We are so familiar with modern humanitarianism, that we are in danger of forgetting how very modern it is. Not only do we find among primitive savages the practice of killing off old members of the tribe, in order not to be handicapped in warfare or to have the food supply unprofitably used; not only in Greece and Rome was the exposure of infants practised, as a ghastly means of reducing the surplus population; but down through the Christian ages, even to the beginning of the nineteenth century, human life was treated with a levity which to-day seems unimaginable. Scores of trivial offences were punishable by death. Duelling, blood feuds and private warfare were widely prevalent. The sacrifice of men by thousands in dynastic and religious wars was taken as a matter of course. When to-day we read in "Sartor Resartus" the vivid picture of thirty men from the British village of Dumdrudge, meeting in Spain thirty from a French Dumdrudge whom they had never seen before and with whom they had no cause of quarrel, the two parties blowing one another's brains out at the word of command, we forget how very novel was Carlyle's moral recoil and protest, even so recently as the eighteen-thirties. Christendom has always assented with its lips to the doctrine that a man is of more value than many sparrows, but in practice it has held that most men are not really worth much more than a comparatively small number of sparrows. The new feeling, which Carlyle voiced, and which is now practically universal (being shared by everybody except monarchs, diplomatists, international capitalists, militarist philosophers and armament manufacturers), is thus a very recent acquisition; and, while we must guard against foolish exaggerations of it, we yet must not suffer it to be lost or even weakened. Those who agree with M. Maeterlinck are undoubtedly in danger of carrying the horror of suffering to such a point that it will overbear the sense of the sanctity of life.

We turn now to the second class of objections to the Maeterlinck doctrine — those which I have for convenience called ethical. The first of these is that his argument, although limited by him to the question of euthanasia, would undoubtedly justify suicide. It is true that he is talking of the doctor's right to kill, but, on his own showing, this is derivative from the sufferer's right to die. Now, a person who has a right to death has the right to kill himself as well as to be killed by others. If, moreover, intense bodily suffering can give this right, it is unthinkable that mental anguish, often much more unendurable, would not equally confer it. There is thus no question but that M. Maeterlinck has given his sanction to far more than he probably intended. There is no logical halting-place between his position and that of the late Robert Ingersoll. Both take a stand which, consciously or unconsciously, is based upon the extremest individualism, and both deny, whether wittingly or not, that there is anything absolute or unconditionally binding in morality. Neither takes any account of the duty of the sufferer, or of the services which, during and even because of his suffering, he may be able to render.

To prove this, I will quote a number of sentences from Colonel Ingersoll's letters and newspaper interviews on the question "Is Suicide a Sin?" [1]

> Under many circumstances a man has the right to kill himself. When life is of no value to him, when he can be of no real assistance to others, why should a man continue? . . .
> So when a man has committed some awful crime, why

[1] These quotations are taken from volume VII of the Dresden edition of Ingersoll's works, published by C. P. Farrell, New York, in 1900. The italics are mine.

should he stay and ruin his family and friends ? Why should he add to the injury ? . . .

Why should a man, sentenced to imprisonment for life, hesitate to still his heart ? The grave is better than the cell. *Sleep is sweeter than the ache of toil.* The dead have no masters.

Mr. Ingersoll proceeds to defend the suicide against the charge of cowardice. He admits that such a man may lack moral courage, but maintains that he displays a high degree of physical bravery. He then continues as follows: —

If men had the courage, they would not linger *in prisons, in almshouses, in hospitals ;* they would not bear the pangs of incurable disease, the sense of dishonour; they would not live in filth and want, *in poverty and hunger,* neither would they wear the chain of slavery. All this [*sic*] can be accounted for only by the fear of death, or "of something after." . . .

When there is no fear of the future, when death is believed to be a dreamless sleep, men have less hesitation about ending their lives.

He then goes on to denounce the law of New York State which made the attempting of suicide a crime. Of this law he says, with one of his ridiculous rhetorical flourishes, that it was "born of superstition, passed by thoughtlessness, and enforced by ignorance and cruelty." In a later utterance, speaking of a man dying of cancer, he writes: —

This man, suffering agonies beyond the imagination to conceive, is of no use to himself. His life is but a succession of pangs. *He is of no use to his wife, his children, his friends or society.*

It will be seen that Mr. Ingersoll's doctrine is very far-reaching. Unlike M. Maeterlinck, he issues his plenary indulgence not only to the hopeless invalid, but to the criminal, the man sentenced to lifelong imprisonment, the inmate of the almshouse or the hospital, and, apparently without any reservation, to all victims of poverty and hunger, filth and want. It is difficult to speak restrainedly of such a teaching; yet it is necessary to do so, since much of this seems, however undesignedly, to be implied in the teaching of M. Maeterlinck, whom I respect, and would seek to turn from the error of his ways.

The first point to be noted is that suicide is, in the great majority of cases, a retreat from evils which one ought to stay and fight. It was so in the teaching of Seneca. This man, one of the purest moralists who ever lived, submitted to the tyranny of Nero because he clung to the thought that he could at any time escape by means of suicide (as he ultimately did) when that tyranny became unendurable. He laid down, as explicitly as Mr. Ingersoll, the doctrine that a man has always the right to choose the time and manner of his death: —

To death alone it is due that life is not a punishment; that, erect beneath the frowns of fortune, I can preserve my mind unshaken and master of itself. I have one to whom I can appeal. I see before me the crosses of many forms. . . . I see the rack and the scourge, and instruments of torture adapted to every limb and to every nerve; but I also see Death. She stands beyond my savage enemies, beyond my haughty fellow-countrymen. *Slavery loses its bitterness when by a step I can pass to liberty.* . . .

Wherever you look, there is the end of evils. You see that yawning precipice — there you may descend to liberty. You see that sea, that river, that well — liberty sits at the bottom. . . . Do you seek the way to freedom? — you may find it in every vein of your body.

Depart from life as your impulse leads you, whether it be by the sword, or the rope, or the poison creeping through the veins; go your way and break the chains of slavery. Man should seek the approbation of others in his life; his death concerns himself alone. That is the best which pleases him most. . . . The eternal law has decreed nothing better than this, that life should have but one entrance and many exits. Why should I endure the agonies of disease, and *the cruelties of human tyranny*, when I can emancipate myself from all my torments and shake off every bond? For this reason, but for this alone, life is not an evil — that no one is obliged to live. The lot of man is happy, because no one continues wretched but by his fault. If life pleases you, live. If not, you have a right to return whence you came.[1]

The phrases which I have italicized prove my contention. Instead of enduring slavery because by a step he could pass to liberty, instead of submitting to the cruelties of human tyranny because it was in his power

[1] These passages, from various writings of Seneca, are collected by Lecky, in his *History of European Morals*, vol. I, chap. 2.

to emancipate himself, Seneca ought to have organized an opposition to slavery, and a revolution against the insane barbarities of Nero. He ought to have inspired a public opinion which would have made these things impossible, instead of teaching a doctrine of submission, and making it endurable by showing the victims of tyranny how they could escape. No great social evil would ever have been rectified if men had taken the line merely of averting its consequences to themselves instead of determining to abolish its cause.

It is peculiarly strange that Colonel Ingersoll (who evidently had got his inspiration from Seneca in this matter) should have omitted to notice that in sanctioning suicide, he was doing the very thing which he had always emptied the vials of his wrath upon Christian theologians for doing. These men had used the doctrine of immortality as an anæsthetic. Throughout the centuries they had reconciled the poor to poverty, and women to degradation and moral outrage, by the teaching of an eternity of bliss which was to compensate for the evils of the present life. Nobody ever denounced this teaching more fiercely than Robert Ingersoll. He was quite right to do so; and it cannot be doubted that the complete change of attitude in regard to this matter which we see in many churches to-day, is in some measure due to his fiery eloquence. How, then, could he fail to see that in advising people to escape by suicide from remediable evils, he was doing the very thing which he had always denounced?

To offer a dreamless sleep to persons who long to be relieved from suffering is morally identical with offering heavenly bliss. Indeed, Mr. Ingersoll's offer is just as much an unwarrantable assumption of knowledge as the theologians'. Nor does the so-called agnostic escape in this matter without falling into open and flagrant self-contradiction. His argument is a perpetual alternation of dogmatism and denial. In one breath he admits that he cannot affirm or deny immortality; in the next, he dogmatically denies it by calling death a dreamless sleep. What supernatural revelation had come to this rejector of the supernatural? Who told him that death is a dreamless sleep? By calling it so he exactly duplicates the blunder of the theologian in dogmatizing about things of which he knows nothing.

My argument, however, in no wise stands or falls by any conclusion we may come to on the question of personal continuance after death. Whether death be a dreamless sleep or the gate of a larger life, it still would remain true that our duty is to resist and overcome evils, not to run away from them. The downfall of Rome was due in part to the fact that such men as the Stoics and the great jurists acquiesced in social atrocities which they ought to have combated. The long arrest of Christian civilization was due to a similar resignation on the part of those who could have been the pioneers of better things. Seneca's teaching, that man is happy solely because he can run away from his evils, is as demoralizing as the ecclesiastical doctrine that we may not resist divinely-ordained royal scoundrels, and that we are to reconcile ourselves to their barbarities by thinking of compensations to come in a life hereafter.

Equally strange is the moral blindness displayed by Colonel Ingersoll in his reiterated assertion that the sufferer from an incurable disease is "of no use" to himself, his wife, his children or society. Universal experience demonstrates that human wisdom and insight are so intensified by suffering that he who has endured most can give the wisest counsel to others. "To have suffered much is like knowing many languages. Thou hast learned to understand all, and to make thyself intelligible to all." Mr. Ingersoll fell into the vulgar error of thinking that a human being can only be of "use" when he can do bodily work, or, at all events, such mental work as necessitates physical activity. He forgot that the most profoundly significant deeds in human life are those that we do with our minds and with our tongues. A word spoken at a solemn moment may be a mightier force for good or ill than any bodily act whatever. Iago was only a talker; Socrates and Jesus did little but speak. Who has not known of sufferers from incurable disease who, by their serenity under pain, and their wise counsel to those about them, have been a benediction to mankind?

On Maeterlinck's and Ingersoll's principles, Captain Scott and his two companions, instead of awaiting death by starvation, would have been entirely justified in precipitating the end. Their fate was a thousand-fold more certain than that of the most hopeless invalid is to the most experienced physician. The odds against their rescue were literally as infinity to one. Prudence, and the philosophy which Ingersoll borrowed from Seneca, would alike have dictated self-slaughter. Yet, because they abstained, and because they endured to the end, they have rendered a service to mankind for all time, which is of more value than all the other results of their expedition combined.

It is a mere vulgarity to say, even in the case of a man dying of cancer, that he is of no use to himself or others. I have known more than one such case in which the character of the sufferer, through his suffering, became ever more serene and radiant, so that he gave such a gift of example and counsel to the watchers at his bedside that their own lives were transfigured thereby. The preciousness of this influence was such that neither the man himself at the time, nor the onlookers in their subsequent retrospect, would have been willing to curtail by a single hour the sufferer's existence. A noble death-bed is one of the most potent and exalting of spiritual influences; yet not through the fact of death, but through the fact of suffering worthily borne, and of spiritual power displayed in spite of it.

Both Maeterlinck and Ingersoll exhibit a singular psychological ignorance in their contention that the refusal to hasten death is due to the survival of religious terror. The roots of this prejudice, says Maeterlinck, "go down to the unacknowledged fears left in the heart by religions that have long since died out in the intelligence of men." So far is this from the truth, that the sense of the sanctity of life is strongest of all in those who are most completely dehypnotized and freed from superstitious doctrines and from the terrors they engender. In the Middle Ages, just as in China to-day, contempt for life and readiness to inflict death were at their maximum when superstition was most rampant. And among the thinkers of Pagan antiquity, it is precisely those who are most completely raised above these irrational terrors, who repudiate the notion of a man's right to forsake his post. It is the clear-eyed and fearless Aristotle who declares that the suicide acts unjustly not to himself, but to the State. It is Socrates whose free soul instinctively recoils from the idea of self-slaughter,—Socrates, who is serenely convinced that no evil can befall a good man either in life or after death, and who discourses at large of the sacred mysteries of the soul, while he is awaiting the execution of that unjust sentence which condemned his judges more surely than it condemned him. The objection of Socrates to suicide is an expression of the deep moral instinct in him. When Cebes asks why suicide is held not to be right, the keen, ready-witted dialectician is at a loss for a rational answer. He cannot say why, "when a man is better dead, he is not permitted to be his own benefactor." He accordingly falls back upon mystical language: —

> There is a doctrine uttered in secret, that man is a prisoner who has no right to open the door of his prison and run away; this is a great mystery, which I do not quite understand. Yet I too believe that the gods are our guardians, and that we are a possession of theirs.[1]

It is entirely consistent with mysticism, as I have above defined it, that a man should sometimes trust his moral intuitions before his intellect has furnished him with a logically coercive justification of them. I do not think, however, that in taking our stand with Socrates, we are cut off from giving a better reason for our ethical instinct than he furnishes in his reply to Cebes. We can, I believe, translate his mystical language into ethical terms. That doctrine uttered in secret, that man is a prisoner who has no right to open the door of his prison and run away, and that we are a possession of our guardians the gods — what does it mean when reduced to terms of experience? It means that man is under obligations which are unconditional. It means that we are the trustees and depositaries of the highest and divinest thing in the universe. Self-conscious rationality exists in us, and, so far as we know, in us alone. When we remove it in ourselves or others, we are false not merely to ourselves, our families, and our nation, and not even merely to hu-

[1] Plato's *Phædo* (Jowett's translation).

manity at large; we are traitors to the universe, deserters from the cosmic army.

Suicide was permitted under the Roman law, and cases are on record of men obtaining explicit permission from the Emperor to resort to it. Yet its prevalence forced Hadrian to treat attempts at suicide on the part of soldiers as equivalent to desertion, and to punish them accordingly. The Emperor was more poetically inspired than he knew. The only metaphor that adequately expresses the position of man in this life is that which likens him to a soldier already enlisted in an army, and therefore pledged in honour to accept without question the main ends for which the army exists, and not to abandon his duty until he is authoritatively released. The army is the army of humanity; its flag is the flag of the world; its uniform is the physical frame we bear, and the rational and moral nature which the whole of humanity has transmitted to each of us.

The moral blindness which I have complained of in Ingersoll, finds its explanation in the fact, patent to all who read him closely, that he was every whit as much obsessed by the traditional theology as were the theologians whom he attacked, although, of course, in a different manner. Just as they always thought in what are called theological terms, so he always thinks in what are called anti-theological terms. Just as they find the sanction for morality in the alleged will of their supernatural deity, so he argues that, since there is no supernatural revelation, there is no basis for any duty which conflicts with a man's apparent self-interest. This is why he falls into the utter absurdity of saying that, in the case of a suicide, "he is to bear the injury, if it be one." His anti-theological animus blinds him to the glaring fact that of all human injuries the most insupportable is that which the suicide inflicts upon his relations. Let those who have borne this burden testify whether they would not sooner die ten deaths, or lose by natural bereavement their ten dearest connections, than suffer the mingled horror and disgrace of having a wife or husband, parent or child, commit suicide. To the pain of the loss is added the unutterable shame of an implied reproach which, however undeserved, can seldom be proved to others, or even to the bereaved themselves, to have been so.

There are some who have no more belief in the scheme of traditional theology than has M. Maeterlinck or than had Colonel Ingersoll, yet who have a deeper sense than they of the sanctity of this life, and of the unconditional nature of the claim of duty upon our allegiance. The question for them is not whether we live after death, or whether the abandonment of life is an offence against a superhuman personality. The question is as to the moral effects upon others of our acts in this life, and as to the way in which we best can discharge the obligations under which each of us has been laid by society, from the very foundation of the human world.

There are those, indeed, who deny the existence of duty. They maintain that, as we do not choose to come into this life and are not consulted as to the circumstances under which we are born, there can be no such thing as a general claim of humanity upon our loyalty. This position implies that a man has a right to get all he can out of life and to give back as little as possible in return. It is a doctrine that cannot be logically refuted. The man who affirms it can only be asked to open his eyes and look somewhat more steadily at the facts of life than he has hitherto done. He must be asked to imagine what would happen to him if society at large acted towards him upon his own principle. He may perhaps, especially in youth, in this individualistic and self‑reliant America, feel strong enough to stand against the world; he forgets, however, that even the bodily strength and the mental shrewdness by which he feels able to do this are things which human society has bestowed upon him. He did not (as he has himself argued) make himself. He therefore, by his own reasoning, is not the owner of himself. That trick of chop-logic by which he denies the brotherly bond of mankind is but the flourish of a borrowed sword. And since for him there are no duties but only rights, then human society has no duties towards him, but only rights which it may enforce against him. To put the point even in the terms of a cash bargain, can any individual person pretend that he has given to mankind value for value in return for what he has received?

But we have admitted that the question cannot be settled by argument. Either the validity of the claim of duty becomes self-evident when fairly presented, or else there is some moral abnormality in the man to whom it is not so. I cannot prove to such a man that when he sees a child drowning, he is bound to do what in him lies to save it. I can, however, tell him that he ought to need no argument on this point, and that the very fact that he needs one is a proof of his own perversion. I cannot, by reasoning, show the coerciveness of the principle, "Inasmuch as ye have done it unto the least of these my brethren, ye have done it unto me." This is, to use old-fashioned language, the logic of the heart, not of the head. "Le cœur a ses raisons, que la raison ne connait pas." We are here dealing with the ultimate facts of our moral constitution. We discover, when the exigency arises, that we are built this way, and that, like Luther, we can do no other. Happily, even those men who assert in words that they do not feel this unconditional imperative of conscience, and who ordinarily live in accordance with the diabolical principle they proclaim, are often as blind to their own nature as to that of others; and generally, when some unforeseen appeal is made to the latent good in them, they find themselves acting by the law which they have repudiated.

The doctrine that suicide is no sin, and that under many circumstances a man has the right to take his own life, is the most dangerously anti-social teaching ever uttered. Nor are its dangers remote or slow to disclose themselves. Ingersoll's utterances on the subject were followed, as everybody remembers, by a perfect epidemic of suicides in the United States. If the misguided man had been a careful student of history, he would have known that the same sequence of events had occurred many times before. Seneca found it necessary to protest against the passion for self-destruction which his own teaching had provoked among his disciples. Cicero tells us of the Cyrenaic philosopher Hegesias, whose teaching had earned him the sobriquet of "the orator of death," and whose eloquent pictures of the fascinations of the tomb led multitudes to free themselves by suicide from the cares of life.

It is curious to observe the astonishing self-contradiction and self-stultification to which Ingersoll was driven when asked whether his teaching had not caused many people to take their lives. He replied, "People do not kill themselves because of the ideas of others." On another occasion, in answer to a similar question, he said, "Talk as long as language lasts, you cannot induce a man to kill himself. The man who takes his own life does not go to others to find reasons or excuses."

That is to say, this man, who all his life had denounced the wrong deeds to which people have been led by false teaching, was driven to deny the connection between teaching and practice when confronted with the horrors which his own mad doctrine had let loose upon the world! If it were true that people's conduct is unaffected by the doctrine and counsel of teachers whom they respect, then all the diatribes of Ingersoll about the horrible results of orthodox theological teaching would be absurd. The reason why they are not so, however, is that there is a real, natural and inevitable connection between teaching and practice. Men imitate one another's deeds, but even stronger is the impulse which leads them to act upon one another's counsel. The Smithfield crowds in Queen Mary's day assisted or acquiesced in the burning of Protestants for no other reason than that they had been taught that heresy was the worst of crimes, and that it was accordingly just that the heretic should be burned. The disciples of Seneca committed suicide because their revered teacher had sanctioned the practice. And Ingersoll was as directly responsible (though, of course, less intentionally so) for the fate of the deluded wretches whose bodies were found with his publications in their pockets, as Mrs. Emmeline Pankhurst and her colleagues were for the insensate outrages which postponed the political emancipation of women in England.

It is commonly maintained to-day, particularly by Christian apologists, that the deep-seated horror of the European mind in regard to self-destruction is a result of the ecclesiastical teaching. Such thinkers point to the contrast in this matter between Europe and the East. They ask why it is that life is held so lightly in China, where a man will commit suicide on your doorstep as a means of insulting you, whereas in Europe the most ghastly symbolism was resorted to in order to express the horror evoked in the mind of society by such an act. We are told that the burial of the suicide in unconsecrated ground, at the cross-roads, and with a stake driven through his body, expressed a mental attitude engendered by Christianity. But I have yet to learn where in the Bible there is any overt and explicit condemnation of the laying of violent hands upon oneself. Hamlet's notion that the Everlasting had "fixed his canon 'gainst self-slaughter" is certainly a part of the European tradition which was caught up and transmitted by the theologians; but Hamlet would not have been able to find the canon in question in the Jewish or Christian Scriptures. Instead, then, of saying that it was Christianity which made Europe condemn suicide, the statement should be precisely inverted: it was the normal healthy instinct of Europe which made Christianity condemn it. In this fashion Christianity has been held responsible for many things, both good and bad, which in truth form no part of it. It is thus, for example, that the claim is made to-day that Christianity emancipated women and led to the abolition of slavery, despite the glaring facts that the most horrible and oppressive laws against women, which still survive in Germany and England, were passed by Christian legislatures, and that every Christian nation practised slavery for centuries, — in some cases, down to a century or two ago. I am not in the least maintaining that slavery, or the degradation of women, or suicide, is consistent with or enjoined by the teaching of Jesus Christ. I am only drawing attention to the fact that between his teaching and that of official Catholicism and Protestantism there is almost always a great gulf fixed. It was not Christianity that forbade self-destruction. It was the instinctive aversion of humanity to the ultimate disloyalty against itself. For this aversion, no doubt, theology found reasons. It has been said that "metaphysics is the finding of bad reasons for what we believe upon instinct." Unquestionably this is true of theology, which has hitherto shown a genius for finding the lamest of reasons for the best of man's instinctive desires and aversions.

The strongest ethical reason against suicide is that suggested by Kant's celebrated criterion. We have to ask ourselves what would happen if everybody acted on the principle on which we propose to act, since a morally sound rule is one which would produce beneficent results if universalized. Apply this canon to the doctrine of Ingersoll, and we see at once that it would lead to the extinction of human society. Every man and every woman sometimes reaches a point where to die seems better than to live. It is not given to the sons of men to pass through life without experiencing moments (and happy are they to whom such moments are rare) when Time seems, to use Tennyson's words, "a maniac scattering dust, and Life a Fury slinging flame." If, at such moments, all men and women were convinced of the truth of Ingersoll's idea, every life would end by suicide. The self-destroyer, says Ingersoll, is not a coward. Even so, few men and women are so cowardly as to be incapable of his act, if they share not only his provocation but his principle of conduct. If Francis Thompson in his outcast days, if Abraham Lincoln, groaning through long years beneath a burden such as few men have ever sustained, if Shakespeare, in that period of spiritual gloom which, according to some critics, gave birth to his greatest tragedies, — if these had shared the horrible individualistic illusion that a man has the right to choose his own time and manner of exit from the world, it is self-evident how ruinous would have been the loss inflicted on mankind.

Our conclusion, then, is the simple ethical rule that a man should never hasten his departure so long as by deed or word or look he can influence for good the character or the circumstances of any fellow-mortal. It is never certain that one cannot do this, and consequently the conditions postulated as justifying suicide can never obtain. But, in formulating our rule, we have furnished ourselves with no excuse for judging harshly of those pitiable souls who violate it. The more a man is impressed with the imperative claim of duty upon himself, the more must he strive to avert or cure those blinding misfortunes which overbear the reason and conscience of others, and impel them to the last disloyalty. The bare statement of the ethical rule may indeed sound harsh, but we may point out that it is tempered by another practical law which should always be remembered in connection with it — namely, that we are to make for others extenuating explanations which we may not make for ourselves. Every suicide is an indictment of the providence of society, and we are bound to feel that we share the guilt of all who, finding life unendurable, take refuge in self-slaughter. The modern world is challenged by an ever-increasing number of such cases. In Germany and England, during the last half-century, the percentage of self-murders has hugely increased in every decade. To show the enormity of the offence is but one of the steps that are necessary to cure the evil. The other and the greater task is to remove all those preventable conditions which combine to produce it.

CHAPTER VIII

THE VICTORIOUS DEATH OF CAPTAIN SCOTT

THE story of the expedition made by Sir Robert Falcon Scott and his companions to discover the South Pole and to increase our scientific knowledge of the Antarctic region, is one that mankind will not willingly let die. I shall here give only a brief résumé of its leading incidents, partly because the facts are so familiar, but chiefly in order that I may devote my space to a consideration of certain trains of ethical thought which the theme suggests.

The question, *Cui bono?* in connection with polar exploration is hard to answer to the satisfaction of those who think of "good" only in commercial-utilitarian terms. But it will never be asked by those whose ideal is the heroic adventurer, not the prudent huckster. Of every exploring party, from the days of the Argonauts to those of Amundsen, Peary and Scott, it has been possible to say beforehand that its risks were great and certain, its gains problematical and perhaps non-existent. Columbus spent years in the attempt to convince men that the only answer to this contention must be, "Try it and see." Imprudent or not, it was inevitable in the nature of man that he should not cease from spying out his planetary domain until he had penetrated the last fastnesses of the un-known. Nor was it any more improbable antecedently that something of surpassing worth should be await-ing man amid the eternal snows than that Columbus should blunder on this continent, mislaid from eter-nity among the wastes of the western sea. Experience alone could decide either question. We dismiss, then, the notion that the Scott party and their equally ill-fated predecessors of the Southern and the Northern night were vainly sacrificed to a gainless quest. In the preceding chapter we have insisted that a man has no right to take his own life. But nobody can deny that under many circumstances one has a right — and often a duty — to risk it; and in our comfort-worship-ping age, it is good to have it proved to us that men can still endure hardness for unselfish ends.

To estimate aright the gallantry of Scott and his colleagues, we must make some attempt to imagine what is involved in spending a year and a half in the utter desolation and the pitiless climate of the great Ice Barrier and the Beardmore Glacier. We who live in the comfort of civilization cannot do justice to this feature of polar exploration. But we can perhaps form some faint conception of the suffering it entails if we imagine ourselves living in canvas tents, for months and months on end, in the fiercest winter weather of the North-Western States.

This, however, is the experience shared in common by all polar explorers. What impresses one in the case of the Scott expedition is the almost supernaturally bad luck which dogged their footsteps at every turn. The collapse of the motor sledges was the first of these incidents. Then their pony transport failed them much earlier than they had anticipated; and then they seem to have given up their dogs sooner than was necessary. The actual polar party, consisting of five men, had to tug a heavy sledge hundreds of miles to the Pole, only to be confronted, on arrival there, by the heart-freezing disappointment of finding that they had been anticipated.

Their return journey was hindered by blizzard after blizzard; and in the significant words of Scott, "we had not one completely fine day," is contained a sufficient explanation of the ultimate tragedy.

Then comes the record of the collapse and death of Petty Officer Evans, "the strongest man of the party." The little company is now reduced to four men, all worn by toil to the verge of collapse, and one of them already marked for death. They are hindered in their progress by the ever - worsening illness of Captain Oates, who at last, unwilling to be a burden upon them, decides to lay down his life. Inexpressibly moving is the brief record, penned by Scott's dying hand, of his companion's heroism. After camp is pitched, and when the blizzard is raging, Oates quietly says, "I am just going outside; I may be some time." If this vicarious death was suicide, it was the one suicide of which I have ever heard that seems completely justified. The cenotaph erected to commemorate the death of Oates expresses in briefest form the intuitive homage of humanity to such a self-sacrifice: "Hereabouts died a very gallant gentleman."

Imagination reels in the effort to follow the march of the three survivors to their final camp, where they arrived with food for two days, but with fuel for only one meal. They were but eleven miles from plenty and comparative safety; but they might as well have been a thousand. They were surrounded by a blizzard which made further progress impossible, even had they been sufficiently fed; and Scott's last message is written after they have been in their tent four days, and when they must, therefore, have been at least two days without food. The pitiless gale was still raging when the dying hand indited its last message to the world. What happened afterwards can only be inferred from the condition of the tent when at last it was discovered by the rescue party. The bodies of Wilson and Bowers were wrapped in their sleeping-bags; that of Scott was outside of his. Evidently he had been able to give this last attention to his friends between the time of their death and his own.

One gathers the character of Scott, not only from the mere list of events in the expedition, but from many little indications disclosed by his diary. First it stands on record that before leaving for the Antarctic he had arranged that the profits on his book should all be divided among his companions, after their return. He had not told them of this arrangement; the money was to come to them in the shape of a surprise bonus.

It is to be remembered, also, that the last message of Scott is the only part of his diary which was consciously written for others to read. The diary itself consists of matter which he must naturally have expected to revise before publication. We may fairly assume, therefore, that it contains a real disclosure of his thought and feeling, uncoloured by adaptation to the tastes or expectations of readers. It was written for the most part when the apparition of failure and death was not present to his mind. We may thus expect to obtain by reading it, and by reading between its lines, a more than ordinarily reliable impression of the character of the writer.

One notes with interest the unaffected regret which Scott expresses on each occasion when he has to send back some of the members of his party. For all of those to whom the favour of participation in the final enterprise could not be extended, he has words of genuine sympathy.

Another characteristic of the man is his repeated rejoicing in the harmony which prevailed among his party, and in their loyalty to himself as leader. He scarcely ever mentions his own share in the work. Yet it lies on the surface of the narrative that the loyalty and harmony, for which he is so grateful, must have been inspired by his own rare personal qualities. We hear much of the unfailing ingenuity of Petty Officer

Evans; the debt of the expedition to the keen eyes of Bowers is repeatedly commemorated. There is enthusiastic praise of the wonderful expedition made by Wilson, Bowers and Cherry-Garrard, to the emperor penguin rookery at Cape Crozier. Scott waxes eloquent in his description of the labour and suffering undergone by his companions in a portion of the expedition in which he did not participate; but there is no record of the even greater trials and torments which he must himself have endured, apart altogether from the tremendous burden of responsibility which inevitably fell to the leader's share.

Still another indication of Scott's calibre is given in his account of the overwhelming disappointment which awaited them at the Pole itself. Here again, although the blow fell heaviest upon him, his only thought is for others: "It is a terrible disappointment, and I am very sorry for *my loyal companions*." We find no trace of jealousy or resentment against his successful rival; only a generous testimony to the efficiency of that rival's work: "There is no doubt that our predecessors have made thoroughly sure of their mark, and fully carried out their programme."

The finest fragment of unconscious self-portraiture, however, which this journal gives us is contained in that last moving message to the public, which the starved and dying man penned at the moment of utter defeat. From his tent amid the eternal desolation, with the last flames of life burning low, he writes, "I do not regret this journey. . . . We took risks; we knew we took them. Things have come out against us, and therefore we have no cause for complaint, but bow to the will of Providence, determined still to do our best to the last." Then, with characteristic self-forgetfulness, "Had we lived, I should have had a tale to tell of the hardihood, endurance and courage of *my companions*, which would have stirred the heart of every Englishman." And, last of all, that appeal to his country's generosity, on behalf of the dependents of his companions and himself, which could not have failed to move the heart of any nation.

One's first reaction upon reading such a narrative is a feeling of proud and joyous confidence in the eternal fineness and dignity of the human spirit. It is in the midst of unrelieved tragedy, it is in the very heart of the triumphs of evil, that we find the refutation of pessimism. When I first read the message of Captain Scott, there sprang up at once in my mind the classic lament of Burke over the decay of the knightly spirit; and, together with it, the glad consciousness that Burke had spoken falsely. Let us recall his familiar words, in order that we may see how completely, even to detail, the story of Scott refutes them: —

> The age of chivalry is gone. That of sophists, economists and calculators has succeeded; and the glory of Europe is extinguished for ever. Never, never more shall we behold that generous loyalty to rank and sex, that proud submission, that dignified obedience, that subor-

dination of the heart, which kept alive, even in servitude itself, the spirit of an exalted freedom. The unbought grace of life, the cheap defence of nations, the nurse of manly sentiment and heroic enterprise, is gone! It is gone, that sensibility of principle, that chastity of honour, which felt a stain like a wound, which inspired courage whilst it mitigated ferocity, which ennobled whatever it touched.[1] . . .

It is characteristic of pessimists to disregard the good in human things. They concentrate attention on exceptional evil, and forget that it is exceptional. They forget that if truth, honesty and justice were not already dominant in large measure, the daily life of human society would be rendered impossible. The heroism of Scott, while its context of tragic circumstance enables it to stand as a typical refutation of Burke's lament, discloses only an exceptional degree of a quality which is common to all mankind, and discernible in the daily history of every group of human beings. There are always courage, self-abnegation and readiness for death in the service of others, even among the poorest and least fortunately circumstanced of mankind. The height of the wave is evidence, to the initiated, of the depth of the ocean from which it springs; and the individual character of such a man as Scott implies and testifies to the presence of his great qualities in the reservoir of spiritual life from which his own being was drawn.

[1] Burke, *Reflections on the Revolution in France.*

Two main lines of reflection are suggested by the incident which we are here considering. The first of these concerns the attitude of the modern world towards death.

It is unquestionable that our thoughts nowadays are far less directed towards death than were those of mankind in the Middle Ages. For then the whole of life was consciously viewed as a preparation for death, and for that larger life which was believed to lie beyond. It was one of the great changes in the human outlook which accompanied the revival of learning, the outburst of the spirit of geographical discovery, and the emergence of the scientific spirit, that the centre of attention was removed to earth, and to the life that now is. In the writings of Bacon, the incarnation of the spirit of science, we find many protests against the morbid focussing of attention on the end of life, which had prevailed down to his time. He points out, with his usual keen psychologica' insight, that there is scarcely any motive in human nature so weak but that it can overcome the fear of death. He further affirms that most of the teachings of philosophers and divines had increased the dread of death, while they offered to cure it; "for, when they would have a man's whole life to be but a discipline or preparation to die, they must needs make men think that death is a terrible enemy, against which there is no end of preparing."

Spinoza, again, voices the growing protest of his age against a gloomy and excessive contemplation of man's mortality. "The free man," he writes, "thinks of nothing so little as of death, and his wisdom is a meditation not of death but of life."

The modern world has passed to an opposite extreme from that of the Middle Ages. Far from needing the advice of Bacon and Spinoza, we need rather to return to something of that seriousness of mind which made the preparation for death an essential part of the business of life. Our attitude to-day is perhaps best expressed in the words of W. K. Clifford: "That love of action which would put death out of sight, is to be counted good, as a holy and healthy thing, necessary to the life of men, serving to knit them together, and to advance them in the right."

Whether this be sound advice or not, it is undeniable that it reflects the actual practice of mankind. But is there not a profounder wisdom? Is there not a middle course between the mediæval brooding over death, and the modern anxiety to forget it? Clifford was a brave spirit, whose early demise was a grievous loss to mankind: and it is with no desire to reflect upon him that I criticize his counsel in this matter. But there seems something shallow, something even of what is called Dutch courage, in the policy of putting death out of sight. It reminds one somehow of that wave of the arm by which Mr. Podsnap was wont to banish into oblivion anything repugnant to the great Victorian English god of comfort and bourgeois respectability.

If Spinoza is right in asserting that the free man

thinks of nothing so little as of death, it can only be in the sense that the free man has already thought out to the end the prospect of death, and made his peace with it. Only then is he truly free — only then can he afford not to think of it; just as the athlete, who has undergone thorough training, need not trouble himself with the question of his fitness when the hour of the struggle comes.

We, to-day, are in general far removed from this high freedom. We have put death out of sight; we have not reconciled ourselves to it. And because we have only banished the spectre but not laid it, we are apt to be smitten with horror at every suggestion of its re-appearance. How many of my readers have ever in their lives devoted ten minutes to meditation on the thought that they too must surrender their being? How many of us have sought in any way to make our peace with death, or to decide whether we loyally accept a life which carries with it, as an inevitable condition, the death of the body? It is our business to think this question out to the end; and only when we have done so, can we be "free men" in the sense of Spinoza.

Various are the ways in which men have made terms with the so-called last enemy. The most common, and the one which probably would still serve the great majority of people, if they seriously considered the subject, is the thought of personal immortality. I cannot here examine this doctrine in detail, and must content myself with remarking that there is an inherent weakness in it from the point of view of our moral and spiritual victory over our lower nature. I am not at the moment raising the question of the truth of the doctrine. It may or may not be the fact that death is the gate of a larger life. My point is that the man who overcomes his fear of death by means of his belief in immortality, has not really vanquished his fear at all. To deny the existence of death, as our Christian Science friends do explicitly, and our orthodox friends implicitly, is not to attain victory over it. There is, indeed, some truth in the bitter words of the satirist who declares that he who finds his refuge in the thought of immortality, has been so completely overcome by the fear of death that he refuses to die on any terms. Spiritual triumph is only attained by the man who is ready for annihilation, and who accepts the gift of life with that stern possibility attached to it.

Another class of men there is, who, irrespective of the thought of immortality, welcome death because they are at outs with life. Complete pessimism falls naturally below what Sir John Seeley called the "suicide-mark." And, short of such despair, it is obvious that world-weariness, or any profound dissatisfaction with the changes and chances of this mortal life, will make a man take comfort in the thought of death merely as an alternative to an existence so unsatisfactory. This is the attitude expressed in the great threnody of Shelley upon the death of Keats. Keats

is happy in that he has escaped the woes inevitable to
man: —

> He is not dead, he doth not sleep,
>   He hath awakened from the dream of life;
> 'Tis we who, lost in stormy visions, keep
>   With phantoms an unprofitable strife,
>   And in mad trance strike with our spirit's knife
> Invulnerable nothings. *We* decay
>   Like corpses in a charnel; fear and grief
> Convulse us and consume us day by day,
> And cold hopes swarm like worms within our living clay.
>
> He has outsoared the shadow of our night.

In like manner, Keats himself welcomes the thought
of dissolution as a refuge from the ills of life. Every
lover of the "Nightingale" Ode knows by heart the
reason why the poet is "half in love with easeful
death." It is because for him this world is a place

> . . . where men sit and hear each other groan,
> Where palsy shakes a few sad, last grey hairs,
>   Where youth grows pale, and spectre-thin, and dies:
>   Where but to think is to be full of sorrow,
>   And leaden-eyed despairs;
>   Where beauty cannot keep her lustrous eyes,
>   Or new love pine at them beyond to-morrow.

The same note of world-weariness rings through
much of our modern poetry. To Swinburne, in some of
his moods, the lot of man seems one of inevitable and
arbitrary frustration. Human aspirations have been
foreordained to failure by the gods from "before the
beginning of years." Thus, in the very spirit of the

Greek tragedians, he pronounces the doom of human striving, in that memorable picture of Man which closes the "Atalanta" chorus: —

> His speech is a burning fire,
>   With his lips he travaileth;
> In his heart is a blind desire,
>   In his eyes foreknowledge of death;
> He weaves, and is clothed with derision;
>   Sows, and he shall not reap;
> His life is a watch or a vision
>   Between a sleep and a sleep.

Death, therefore, is welcome, if not for its own sake or for life's sake, at least as a haven of escape from life: —

> From too much love of living,
>   From hope and fear set free,
> We thank, with brief thanksgiving,
>   Whatever gods may be,
> That no life lives for ever;
> That dead men rise up never;
> That even the weariest river
>   Winds somewhere safe to sea.

And again, in the haunting cadences that close his "Ave atque Vale" to Baudelaire, it is the incurable troublesomeness of life that makes death welcome: —

> Content thee, howsoe'er, whose days are done.
>   There lies not any troublous thing before,
>   Nor sight, nor sound, to war against thee more;
> For whom all winds are quiet as the sun,
>   All waters as the shore.

Probably no more seductive embodiment of the idea under discussion could be found than these poetic pre-

sentations of it which I have quoted; yet, despite the
magic of the poets, we cannot fail to detect the note of
morbidity in their strain. We refuse to assent to the
doctrine that life is inherently and irremediably evil;
and if we can make our peace with death only by embracing this teaching, then with death we must remain
unreconciled. But is there no alternative to the choice
between the hope of immortality and the despair of
this life? Are we shut up to selecting one or the other
of these two horns whereon to impale ourselves?

Not so. There is still another attitude towards
death, which can be adopted by those of us who neither
stake our faith upon the thought of eternal existence
for the individual, nor are willing to stultify our life in
this world by implying that release from it, on any
terms, were better than its continuance. This third
attitude is hinted at by the mediæval Catholic, St.
Francis of Assisi, and is brought out into clear relief in
the ultra-modern American poet of democracy, Walt
Whitman. In his "Canticle of the Sun," St. Francis
gives thanks, with profound insight, for "our sister,
the death of the body." And Whitman, in lines which
are dear to many in the Ethical Movement, who have
known them by heart for years, praises the fathomless
universe as whole-heartedly for "the sure-enwinding
arms of cool-enfolding death" as he does "for life and
joy, and for objects and knowledge curious, and for
love, sweet love." Almost startling in their daring
seizure of what to many is the most piercing of the

thorns of life, are his words of welcome to the ghostly visitant: —

Dark mother, always gliding near with soft feet,
Have none chanted for thee a chant of fullest welcome ?
Then I chant it for thee; I glorify thee above all;
I bring thee a song, that, when thou must indeed come, thou
    come unfalteringly.

Here, surely, is the rare equipoise of sanity and viril-ity. Here is the harmony which we are seeking. It is because the singer is in love with *life* that he welcomes death, the inevitable condition of life. It is because "Life's gift outruns his fancies far" that he is prepared to accept it subject to the proviso that it must end. How far in advance is this of the attitude which would put death out of sight! How much finer, morally and spiritually, than the attitude which considers death only a make-believe, only the entry to a fuller life!

To the reader who has followed me thus far I need not repeat that I do not deny immortality *as a fact*. My attitude towards it is one of suspended judgment. The would-be scientific evidence for it seems to me, as I have shown in an earlier chapter, as futile as the dog-matic materialism which undertakes to prove it impos-sible. My point here is, however, that the man who *de-pends morally* on the hope of immortality, is *ipso facto* morally poorer than he who does not. There is a defect in the cosmic patriotism of one who needs this assurance; and in these days, when men are losing their hold, much more extensively than is generally imagined, upon the

belief in a life hereafter, it becomes increasingly peril-
ous to seek in such a quicksand our moral anchorage.

The only way to true spiritual freedom and to ultimate peace is to regard this life as the sphere of duty,
and to accept duty itself as the supreme and unconditional goal of existence. Such was the depth of moral
insight attained by St. Teresa, who, as the legend goes,
was seen with a lighted candle in one hand, and a
bucket of water in the other, and, being asked what
these were for, replied that she wished to burn up
heaven and to extinguish the flames of hell, in order
that men might love God with a love uncorrupted
either by fear of punishment or by hope of reward.
This heresy of the Catholic saint is an instance of the
finest ethical orthodoxy. If our attitude towards life
be thus centred on the fulfilment of duty, if we regard
this frame of things as having for its final cause the
manifestation of man's highest moral attributes, we
at once obtain a perfectly clear orientation. We are at
once committed to a willing acceptance of life, so long
as it can be made to last; and we shall be equally ready,
when our day closes, to sing with joy what Bacon calls
the sweetest canticle of all, "Now lettest thou thy
servant depart in peace."

The second problem which the fate of Scott forces
us to consider is that of the standard of success in
life. What constitutes success? I put aside entirely
the vulgar materialism which would define it in terms

of cash or of newspaper publicity. I assume that none of my readers needs to be converted from a criterion, the fallacy of which is as obvious as its vulgarity. The question I put to myself is whether even that finer standard, which makes success dependent on the realization of one's conscious aim in life, does not also need revision. That this is the criterion of success adopted by many whose character and whose ethical insight are entitled to our respect, does not, I think, need proving. The defect of such a standard is that it groups among failures those who have given to mankind the very finest and most heroic examples that have irradiated the pathway of history.

Judging by this standard, Robert Scott failed, and Roald Amundsen succeeded. Judging by it, too, martyrdom is inevitably a proof of failure. Yet do we not feel that there is something amiss with a criterion which classes among failures such men as Socrates, Jesus, Sir Thomas More, Hugh Latimer, and Robert Scott, and such a woman as Joan of Arc? In regard to each of these we feel, intuitively, the appositeness of the note of triumph which Milton sounds over the death of Samson, in the "Samson Agonistes": —

> Nothing is here for tears, nothing to wail
> Or knock the breast; no weakness, no contempt,
> Dispraise or blame; nothing but well and fair,
> And what may quiet us in a death so noble.

Yet how can this attitude of exultation be made to consist with the verdict of failure on such lives? Is not such triumphant acclamation the very hall-mark of success?

To return to our modern instance, has not Captain Scott, by the manner of his death, conferred upon humanity something far finer than his triumphant return would have involved? To say this is not to minimize the tragedy of his loss; it is only to insist upon the eternal value which mankind undauntedly extracts from the greatest temporal woes. The spontaneous testimony of our consciousness affirms that the attainment of the South Pole is worth far less, morally, than the explorer's approximation to the high meridian of spiritual triumph. The glory of the Antarctic Midnight Sun is dim indeed, when compared with the "supersolar blaze" of the victory of the soul over the body, and over the hostility of the outward world.

The criterion of success which I would seek to formulate, must give a rational justification to the spontaneous feeling of triumph inspired in us by the heroic death of the martyr. And, upon analysis, our way to formulate such a criterion seems to become clear. It is undeniably a fact that there is in every man and woman something greater than the individual will. Each of us is a transitory incarnation of a universal will, however we may describe it — whether as the will of God or of humanity. Now in the triumph of this greater will — in the fulfilment of the organic law of our spiritual being — there is attained a success far outshining in splendour the achievement of one's conscious personal aim in life. The manifestation, in despite of a hostile world, of those qualities of character which command the immediate admiration of all disinterested observers, constitutes the success of the racial will; and frequently the very condition of this success is the failure of one's conscious purpose. In every case of martyrdom worthy of reverence, from Socrates down to Robert Scott, it is this greater success which accounts for the triumphant exaltation of our hearts in the face of grimmest tragedy. Let us say, then, that *success consists either in fulfilling one's conscious purpose or in exemplifying the organic trend of the general will of man; and only that life is a failure in which neither of these ends is attained.*

Upon the rude monument which marks the last resting place of Scott, Bowers and Wilson, are inscribed the closing words of Tennyson's "Ulysses": "To strive, to seek, to find, and not to yield." The lines which end with these words interpret not only the spirit of the explorer, but the whole history of human advance. They nobly sum up the high adventure of humanity, its æonian striving against incalculable odds:—

> One equal temper of heroic hearts
> Made weak by time and fate, but strong in will
> To strive, to seek, to find, and not to yield.

In the unpathed desolation of the Antarctic snows, cut off for ever from all that he held dear, knowing that he should never see again the face of wife or child, and awaiting the approach of death, Scott was able to say, "I do not regret this journey." May we so live that at the last — in utter desolation, if so it must be — neither we nor they who look to us for example and strength, shall find aught for regret in the tale of our journey through the wilderness of this world.

EPILOGUE

IN THE TIME OF WAR AND TUMULTS

September, 1914

IT will be evident to the reader of the foregoing chapters that they were penned and made ready for publication before the descent of that avalanche of insanity by which at the present moment Europe is overwhelmed. Without venturing upon prophecy, the author cannot refrain from expressing the hope that before these words meet the reader's eye, the war will have become a memory. To write of such matters under such circumstances is in itself difficult and embarrassing; but to one placed as the author is, the difficulty becomes so great that it may well seem an unwarrantable temerity to attempt it at all. On the other hand, silence at such a juncture, in one who had presumed to offer counsel on social and moral issues, might seem an evidence not alone of incompetence but of cowardice.

Although, like all other members of Peace Societies, whether in America, in England or in the European countries, I had long been convinced that the competition in naval armaments between England and Germany, and in military equipment between Germany and her Continental neighbours, must inevitably, at some time, issue in strife, yet the expected, when it befell, seemed to me unexpected and incredible. I little thought, when I landed in England on the first of June last, that before I sailed again for home, I should see my native country transformed as by magic into an armed camp — its intellectual and industrial life in abeyance, its credit system so disturbed that Bank of England notes could with difficulty be exchanged for gold, and the maturing of liabilities had to be deferred by means of a moratorium; its struggle for social justice to the poor and to women arrested, and its party strifes and class antagonisms quelled and replaced by undreamed-of fraternity and singleness of purpose. No layman, uninitiated in the subterranean secrets of diplomacy, could have foreseen that the treasonable talk of civil war in Ireland would so soon be replaced by union between Nationalists and Ulstermen, both patriotically declaring in the House of Commons that they would join in defending the shores of Ireland against invasion from abroad.

The case was the same with the multitude of American tourists who went to taste the fruits of the long centuries of culture-history treasured up in the cities of continental Europe. Not one of them dreamed that his holiday journey would develop into so unprecedented an adventure as for thousands of them it has proved. Protracted security had dulled our imaginations, and, like the dwellers in Messina and in ancient Pompeii, we had forgotten the titanic energies beneath and around us, which could at any moment over-whelm us and plunge the nations into lamentation and mourning and woe.

The failure of the mass of us to anticipate the cata-clysm at this time, however, can scarcely be ascribed to defect of political insight. For all forecasting of the course of human affairs necessarily presupposes the continuance of average sanity among mankind, just as scientific calculation assumes the continuous work-ing of the normal and familiar forces of nature. Like thousands of other Englishmen, I had travelled and studied in Germany, and always, after the first few days of my sojourns there, had well-nigh forgotten that I was not at home. The identity of race, the family connection of speech, the cultural similarity between England and Germany, seemed certain pledges of continuous amity. Never before, through all the stormy centuries, had England and Germany been at strife. The perfect kindliness of my German hosts and friends, the solidarity of interests of individ-uals and classes of both peoples, and of the two na-tions, in their common efforts for the enduring inter-ests of humanity, were so complete that the notion of warfare between them seemed fantastic. Nor was it to be supposed that those responsible for the policy of the two countries could become oblivious to the dem-onstrated fact that no nation, even though victorious, can profit economically by war. These, however, are considerations which it is idle to address to the capitalists of international murder, to emperors drunk with mutual jealousy and lust of power, or to professional militarists aching to apply the skill and the weapons they have mastered.

I will not disobey the wisest voice which has been heard in these distracted times — that of our great and revered President — by seeking to analyze the immediate causes of this war or to apportion the blame for its precipitation. This is not the time, nor am I the man, to cast a verdict which only the calm and fully informed judgment of posterity will be able to render with perfect equity. Yet there are some considerations which even at this moment may serve to comfort the consciences of all who, during the past ten years, have laboured for a policy by which peace could be not only maintained but effectively insured for the future. To me it is a satisfaction to recall that during those years I protested many times in England, by speech and writing, against what seemed the mistaken and dangerous foreign policy of my native country. But the voice of that tiny minority of us which pleaded for a *rapprochement* with Germany, and against the dragging of England at the chariot-wheels of Russia, was as that of one crying in the wilderness. The influence of newspapers openly or covertly seeking to promote the interest of the armament capitalists was sufficiently loud and widespread to drown the voice of humanity and prudence, and to keep public opinion in such a condition that no effective opposition could be raised to Sir Edward Grey's pro-Russian undertakings.

On the other hand, the spirit of impartiality demands the recognition of two facts: first, that the lay world is not in possession of all the data, and that there may have been many reasons for the policy pursued by Sir Edward Grey which it has not yet been possible for him to disclose; and, secondly, that efforts have undoubtedly been made more than once by the British Cabinet to arrive at a basis of understanding with Germany. We must not forget those "unofficial" secret missions undertaken by Lord Haldane — a "good European" if ever there was one; nor can we fail to perceive that obstacles too great for him to overcome must have been formidable indeed.

The outstanding lesson of the immediate situation is the fact that nowhere in the world has democracy as yet attained to the control of foreign policy. Here in America it is mistakenly assumed by most journalists that in this matter there is a great difference between the United States and the monarchies and Kaiserdoms of Europe. The difference, however, is by no means so great as it appears: and for this reason, — that whenever among a group of nations one or two are despotically governed, and conduct their international affairs in secrecy and upon the principles of Machiavelli,[1] it is impossible to have publicity and

[1] Note, for example, the candid admission of Prince von Bülow, in his *Imperial Germany*, that national egoism is the only standard

democratic control of those affairs in any of the other nations. When, several months ago, President Wilson urged the passing of the Panama Tolls Repeal Bill, he told Congress that if that measure were not passed the American Government would be involved in international difficulties of great delicacy and complexity. No ordinary American citizen and no journalist — nay, not even the members of the Senate and House of Representatives — really knew to what he alluded. And certainly that minority of writers in our Press which last spring was clamouring for war with Mexico, and sneering at the Secretary of State for his splendid and successful efforts to avert it, was altogether oblivious of the world - wide conflagration which might easily have been precipitated if their bellicose desires had been granted. Democratic as America is, it is no whit more so than are England and France; and the idea that the mass of the electors here controls the foreign policy of the United States is virtually as complete a delusion as it would be in France or England. The foreign policy of democracies is controlled by the Czars and Kaisers of despotic countries, since these, having the power to make war, can force defensive militarism upon the nations they menace.

Yet the American idea, delusion as it is, defines an

that governs German foreign policy. Remember, too, that in this matter he is only more candid than the statesmen and diplomatists of other nations, since all have acted upon the principle which he confesses. I would refer also to the history of the pan-German movement in Professor Roland Usher's masterly treatise on *Pan-Germanism*. (Boston: Houghton Mifflin Company, 1913.)

ideal. Throughout Europe and America democracy *ought* to do this thing which it is here mistakenly believed that democracy does. One cannot but hope that as a result of this war there will be such an advance towards constitutionalism in Russia, Austria and Germany that the *Weltpolitik* of those three nations will actually be dominated by their electorates. Only then will it be possible for the same kind of control to be actualized in England, France and America. And, step by step with the gradual attainment of this ideal, the following lessons must be learned, and the conditions which they show to be necessary for the maintenance of peace must be brought about: —

(1) Each nation must realize that hitherto the end which every Government has consciously or unconsciously laboured for in international polity has been not the good of its nation as such, but the advantage of capitalists. England fought the Boer War for the benefit of the cosmopolitan financiers who controlled the diamond mines of Kimberley and the goldfields of the Witwatersrand. Behind the Mexican chaos lay perceptibly the conflicting interests of the European and American capitalists of the oil industry. The French people had no concern in the conquest of Morocco; here again it was the desire of capitalists (and not alone French capitalists, but the financiers of all Europe) to exploit the resources of the country which brought about the shedding of blood. Thus has it been until now with the diplomacy of the entire

world; and not one of the wars of recent times — least of all the present war — would have been entered upon, had the decision of international questions been governed by consideration for the interests of nations as such.

It is here that we touch upon the essential weakness of the celebrated argument of Mr. Norman Angell. It is perfectly true, as he contends, that as a whole and in the long run a nation inevitably loses by war, even though it be victorious in the technical military sense. But it is not true that groups of capitalists, representing interests sufficiently strong to enable them at critical moments to sway the balance between peace and war, are bound to lose by the wars which they provoke. International capitalism, as it has developed in Europe and America during the past fifty years, has demonstrated itself to be a thing so soulless that it will always act for the furtherance of its interests, no matter what nation may suffer or be ruined in the process. The democratic *Weltpolitik* of the future is bound to see to it (even though experience should prove that this can only be done by setting up the economic régime of socialism) that these interests shall be deprived of their decisive voice in the settlement of international differences.

(2) The next pre-requisite of a civilized foreign policy must be the abolition of all private trading, both international and intra-national, in armaments and lethal weapons of every description. The nations

of Europe are to-day plying their mutual destruction with weapons which they have made for one another. The cynicism of a firm at Birmingham or Essen exporting, for private profit, weapons which will quite probably be used against Englishmen or Germans, is so inhuman that no adequate characterization of it is possible. Yet, under the hypnotizing idolatry of business in which we are all involved, we have patiently suffered it to go on. Here again, we must remember, the beam is in our own eye as well as in that of Europe. Had there been war between the United States and Mexico, our men would have been shot down with guns supplied to Mexico from America. Now, there is only one way to deal effectually with this situation, and that is by abolishing all private manufacture of and trading in weapons of destruction. Each nation must make this business a national monopoly, and international law must prohibit any nation from supplying any other with armaments. Only in this way can such scandals be obviated as those which were recently brought to light in Germany — where the noble Socialist Liebknecht exposed the corrupt control exercised by the Krupps over the Press and over important departments of the Government — and in Japan, where naval officers have been convicted of receiving bribes, also from the Krupps. I have already alluded to the state of things in England, where influential newspapers are controlled in the sinister interests of the armament monopolists. If there have not been scan-

dals of the same kind in the United States, it is still
notorious that incalculable evil is done here through
private trading in pistols. Schemes of regulation and
licensing cannot prevent this harm so long as private
firms are suffered to have a pecuniary interest in supplying revolvers to anybody who wishes for them. In
Chicago, there is never apparently any difficulty in the
way of a highway robber who wishes to provide himself with the deadly tools of his anti-social business;
the result being that homicides in Chicago are more
than twelve times as frequent as in London. If the
trade in arms were monopolized by the Federal Government, this mountainous scandal — which is so constantly before our eyes that we have become psychi-
cally blind to it — would be rendered impossible.

(3) The objective of all humanitarians who believe in the inviolability of nations should be the
establishment of an effective treaty between America,
Germany, France and England, for the maintenance
of peace among themselves and for its enforcement
throughout the rest of the world. With democratic
control of foreign policy in each of the nations specified, such a scheme would become feasible, utopian as
it may sound at the present moment. These four nations, reinforced as they would be by their colonial
dominions, would represent a force such as no conceivable combination of other powers could dream of
attacking; and the pact might in time be extended
to include Russia. A perfectly impartial court for the

adjudication of international differences — impartial, because it should represent all the nations, small as well as great, with equal delegations — should be established, as also an international police, both by sea and land, sufficient to prevent any aggression as between other nations. No country would venture upon the exploitation of its weaker neighbours if it knew that it would have to encounter the armed forces not only of its victim but of this invincible union of world-powers.

It is idle to say that such a fourfold joining of hands in the cause of peace is impossible. If it were so, the hope of the pacific development of humanity would be a delusion. Such a union requires only that level of common honesty and mutual good faith among nations which already exists, which is the necessary pre-condition of the commerce of the world, and which would have sufficed to prevent the present war in Europe save for that sinister influence of emperors and of armament-mongers which our hypothesis assumes to be eliminated from the future situation.

Amid the clash of those peoples over whom the destroying angel is passing, so that soon, alas! there will be no house where there is not one dead, we in America have cause for unspeakable thanksgiving. We shall prove ourselves unworthy of our high destiny if we suffer the feuds and the estranging hatreds of the Old World to blaze out on our soil. To all Americans of European birth who genuinely give to America their highest loyalty, I, born in England, a candidate for the citizenship of this Republic, offer the hand of fellowship, and this word of comfort in the grief that afflicts us all: Remember that, though *your* countries and *my* country are at war, OUR country is at peace with all mankind. May she preserve her unity, and that nobly disinterested tradition in foreign policy manifested, to the admiration of all Europe, in Cuba and Mexico: so that, when the vials of apocalyptic wrath beyond the seas are spent, she may enter to motion peace — the welcome arbitress of Europe's dissensions, the trusted daughter, first of England, but in lesser degree of all the nations now at strife, called in to cover their shame and to mediate the purgation of their sins.

THE END

The Riverside Press
CAMBRIDGE . MASSACHUSETTS
U . S . A